Impediments to Trade Liberalization in the Philippines

This is the fifth title in the Thames Essay Series, arising out of the Trade Policy Research Centre's programme on the Participation of Developing Countries in the International Trading System, supervised by Martin Wolf, the Centre's Director of Studies. Earlier titles were

Myths and Reality of External Constraints on Development by James Riedel

Economic Impact of Generalized Tariff Preferences by Rolf J. Langhammer and André Sapir

East African Lessons on Economic Liberalization by David Bevan, Arne Bigsten, Paul Collier and Jan Willem Gunning

Developing Countries in the GATT Legal System by Robert E. Hudec

Other titles in the programme to be published as Thames Essays are provisionally entitled

Impediments to Trade Liberalization in Sri Lanka by Deepak Lal and Sarath Rajapatirana

Impediments to Trade Liberalization in Latin America edited by Larry A. Sjaastad

Impediments to Trade Liberalization in the Republic of Korea by Soogil Young

The cartoon by KAL on the cover appeared in *The Economist*, London, on 7 February 1987. In the concluding chapter of this Thames Essay, Romeo Bautista discusses the economic difficulties which President Corazon Aquino and her government have to overcome in the Philippines, following the excesses of the Marcos regime.

Thames Essay No. 54

Impediments to Trade Liberalization in the Philippines

BY

Romeo M. Bautista

Gower
Aldershot · Brookfield USA · Hong Kong · Singapore · Sydney

for the
TRADE POLICY RESEARCH CENTRE
London

First published 1988 by

Gower Publishing Company Limited
Gower House, Croft Road, Aldershot, Hampshire GU11 3HR
United Kingdom

Gower Publishing Company
Old Post Road, Brookfield, Vermont 05036
United States of America

Gower Publishing Australia
85 Whiting Street, Artamon, Sydney, New South Wales 2064
Australia

ISSN 0306-6991
ISBN 0 566 05782 4

British Library Cataloguing-in-Publication Data
Bautista, Romeo M.
Impediments to Trade Liberalization in the Philippines.
(Thames Essay No. 54)
1. Philippines. Foreign Trade
I. Title. II. Trade Policy Research Centre.
III. Series
382'.09599

Library of Congress Cataloging-in-Publication Data
Bautista, Romeo M.
Impediments to Trade Liberalization in the Philippines.
(Thames Essay No. 54)
Bibiliography: p.74
1. Phillipines—Commercial Policy
2. Tariff—Philippines
3. Foreign Trade Promotion—Philippines
4. Philippines—Foreign Economic Relations.
I. Title. II. Series.
HF1599.B38 1988 382.3'09599—dc19 88-11263

Printed in the United Kingdom by
Biddles Ltd, Guildford, Surrey

Contents

Biographical Note

ROMEO M. BAUTISTA, who was Deputy Director-General of the National Economic Development Authority, a part of the Government of the Philippines, from 1979 to 1981, is now a Research Fellow at the International Food Policy Research Institute in Washington. Before his present appointment, he was Professor of Economics at the University of the Philippines in 1978-85, having begun to teach there in 1961. In 1981-82 he was Acting President of the Philippine Institute of Development Studies.

After graduating from the University of the Philippines in 1961, Dr Bautista obtained his masters degree in economics from there in 1966 and was then a Rockefeller Scholar at Yale University, where he obtained his doctorate in 1970. He was subsequently a visiting fellow at the East-West Centre in Honolulu (1972-73), at the National Bureau of Economic Research in New York (1975-76) and at the Research School of Pacific Studies, Australian National University (1977). Dr Bautista has been a consultant to, *inter alia*, the Economic Commission for Asia and the Far East in Bangkok, the United Nations Trade and Development Conference in Geneva and the World Bank in Washington.

Dr Bautista was Editor of the *Philippine Review of Business and Economics* in 1973-75 and 1976-79. He has had numerous articles published in professional journals. He is co-author of

Industrial Promotion Policies in the Philippines (1979) and *Capital Utilization in Manufacturing* (1981), author of *Industrial Policy and Development in the ASEAN Countries* (1983) and editor of *Energy and Structural Change in the Asia-Pacific Region* (1984).

Preface

RELATIONS between developed and developing countries in the international trading system, whose norms, rules and procedures are set out in the General Agreement on Tariffs and Trade (GATT), have been reaching an *impasse*. For quarter of a century, the developed countries have been allowing, or encouraging, the developing countries to become contracting parties to the GATT without requiring them to abide by the more important obligations of membership. What is more, they have acquiesced in the formal derogation from the principle of non-discrimination, which is the keystone of the GATT, to permit the Generalized System of Preferences (GSP) in favour of developing countries to be established and maintained.

At the same time, developing countries — especially the more advanced ones — have been faced with discriminatory protection against them whenever their exports have been uncomfortably successful in the markets of developed countries, such protection often taking the form of export-restraint arrangements negotiated 'outside' the framework of GATT norms, rules and procedures.

The costs to developing countries of limitations on their access to the markets of developed countries are not so much offset as multiplied by their more or less complete freedom to establish and maintain trade regimes which are highly protectionist and Byzantine in their complexity.

By the early 1980s, it was clear that the role of developing countries in the international trading system was bound to attract increasing attention, especially if a new 'round' of multilateral trade negotiations under GATT auspices was to be undertaken. Accordingly, the Trade Policy Research Centre, with the help of a grant from the Leverhulme Trust in London, embarked in 1983 on a major programme of studies on the Participation of Developing Countries in the International Trading System, supervised by Martin Wolf, the Centre's Director of Studies.

The purpose of the programme has been to clarify, for public discussion and policy formation, the underlying reasons for the current difficulties in relations between developed and developing countries in the GATT system. The programme focusses both on economic and legal issues in the GATT system *per se* and on impediments to trade liberalization in individual developing countries. The emphasis on the latter derived from the perception that the GATT framework of norms, rules and procedures can be no more than the 'handmaiden' of trade liberalization. Liberalization will not be brought about, however, unless there is a consensus in the countries concerned on both its feasibility and its value in promoting their economic growth and development. The domestic impediments to trade liberalization have to be understood if they are to be overcome.

It is true for all countries that multilateral negotiations are a means more of achieving the trade liberalization that is already widely understood to be in each country's own interests than of liberalizing when no such benefit is seen. In other words, reciprocal bargaining is a way of overcoming domestic resistance to the trade liberalization that is strongly desired by prevailing forces in each country, both in government and in society at large. A desire to liberalize, almost irrespective of what happens elsewhere, is particularly significant in small countries. The smaller the country, the less effective is its international bargaining power and, therefore, the less persuasive is the argument that improved access to markets abroad depends on the liberalization of access to its own market. For this reason, smaller countries usually liberalize only if there is a strong domestic consensus that such liberalization is in their own interests, such a consensus having been long established in countries like Sweden, Switzerland and Singapore.

From a trade policy point of view, almost all developing countries are small. Thus the use they can or will make of the international trading system depends, in the first place, on the strength of the domestic desire to liberalize and, in the second place, on the role that international bargaining can play in the process. It is with these questions in mind that a number of country studies have been undertaken as part of the Centre's programme. Apart from the study of the Philippines reported in these pages, there are studies of the Republic of Korea and and Sri Lanka in Asia, of Kenya and Tanzania in Africa and of Argentina, Brazil and Colombia in Latin America.

Romeo Bautista, formerly of the University of the Philippines and now at the International Food Policy Research Institute (IFPRI), one of foremost economists of the Philippines, was invited to prepare a study on the impediments to trade liberalization in his country. The Philippines is one of the most interesting cases, because of the difficulty the country has had in achieving and sustaining liberal policies, in spite of a general commitment to private enterprise and the country's location in a region where many of the most outward-looking developing countries are to be found.

Dr Bautista shows that the Philippines has long had a highly protected economy and that this has had much to do with the country's poor performance in comparison with her neighbours. In the early 1970s, however, a large depreciation of the real rate of exchange led to a greatly improved export performance during the decade but this was not enough to prevent a substantial accumulation of external debt. As in many countries in Latin America, this accumulation largely reflects the difficulty experienced by the Government of the Philippines in controlling the budget deficit.

In 1981 a trade liberalization programme of unprecedented

scope was planned. The foreign-exchange crisis of 1983, however, made it necessary to impose foreign-exchange and import controls, signalling an emergency retreat from liberalization. The main reason for the crisis was the combination of the public finance problem at home and the decline in the willingness of international lenders to provide additional funds, following the 'debt crisis' in Latin America.

In retrospect, it is clear that the trade liberalization programme faced two fundamental problems. The first was that it largely reflected an agreement of the World Bank with the Minister-technocrats in the Government of Ferdinand Marcos. There remained substantial political resistance which President Marcos was unable (or unwilling) to overcome. The second was that policies at the macro-economic level conflicted with the goal of liberalization, for they implied an ultimately unsustainable level of foreign borrowing. The new Government of Corazon Aquino is also committed to trade liberalization. If it wishes to succeed where its predecessors have failed, it must provide a real impulse towards trade liberalization and, at the same time, achieve macro-economic stabilization and a concomitant resolution of the debt problem.

Drafts of the papers arising from the Centre's programme of studies were presented at a three-day research meeting at Wiston House, near Steyning, in the United Kingdom, attended by those engaged on the programme and a number of other scholars and officials. The meeting was immediately preceded by a two-day meeting, also at Wiston House, of a study group which is drawing together the conclusions of the programme of studies. This meeting, too, was attended by a number of officials. The two international meetings were funded by a grant from the Ford Foundation in New York, while the programme of studies as a whole has been funded by the Leverhulme Trust in London.

Dr Bautista is grateful for the comments of Richard Snape and Djismand Simandjuntak at the Wiston House meeting. He is also grateful to Martin Wolf and John Mellor, who read carefully the earlier drafts and gave valuable comments and suggestions for improvements.

As usual, it has to be stressed that the views expressed in this Thames Essay do not necessarily represent those of members of the Council or those of the staff and associates of the Trade Policy Research Centre which, having general terms of reference, does not represent a consensus of opinion on any particular issue. The purpose of the Centre is to promote independent analysis and public discussion of international economic policy issues.

HUGH CORBET
Director
Trade Policy Research Centre

London
May 1988

Introduction

Martin Wolf

THE purpose of the programme of studies, of which this study is a part, has been to examine the obstacles to the increased participation of developing countries in the international trading system, as governed by the General Agreement on Tariffs and Trade (GATT). From the beginning, however, it was obvious that the principal obstacle to such participation was the inability and, indeed, the unwillingness of the countries concerned to contemplate a significant reduction in their own trade barriers. For this reason, a major part of the programme has been an examination of obstacles to trade liberalization, both political and economic, in a selected group of developing countries.

The countries included in the programme were Argentina, Brazil and Colombia in Latin America; the Republic of Korea, Sri Lanka and the Philippines in Asia; and Kenya and Tanzania in East Africa. In addition, in 1985 the Trade Policy Research Centre published a study, by T.G. Congdon, of the liberalization experience of countries in the Southern Cone of Latin America, focussing on the interesting and important experience of Chile, a study which is complementary to those appearing in the present programme.[1]

Purpose of the Country Studies

Since the starting point for the programme of studies was the fuller participation of developing countries in the international trading system, as regulated by the GATT, the group of countries selected for study may appear somewhat puzzling. There is very little concern within the GATT system about the policies of relatively small and poor developing countries like Kenya, Tanzania or Sri Lanka. Nobody expects even larger countries like Argentina, Colombia and the Philippines to make significant changes in their policies in the context of mutilateral negotiations such as the Uruguay Round. Indeed, of the countries selected for study, only Brazil and the Republic of Korea are undoubtedly high on the list of those expected by the developed countries to participate more fully in the GATT system or, as it is sometimes put more controversially, to 'graduate'.

There are two major implications of this lack of interest in the policies of most of the countries under analysis. First, one might wish to agrue that participation in the GATT can be the 'handmaiden' of trade liberalization by developing countries, as it has certainly proved to be in the case of the developed countries. More precisely, reciprocal bargaining could be a way of overcoming domestic resistance to trade liberalization, while international obligations could also be a bulwark against subsequent increases in protection. But such a justification for fuller participation in the GATT has only modest force, at best, in the case of most developing countries. One can hardly justify liberalization (or resistance to increases in protection) by reference to international repercussions if the reaction of the international community is going to be yawning indifference. Secondly, as a corollary of this very indifference, developing countries can, individually at least, have little impact on the obligations assumed or actions undertaken by other contracting parties of the GATT (including other developing countries).[2]

The reciprocal bargaining that is at the heart of the process of trade liberalization in the GATT framework is, by its nature, a game played by countries that have something with which to bargain. Small countries must, willy nilly, accept whatever crumbs fall from the negotiators' table. This does not mean, however, that negotiations in the GATT are of little importance for those countries. A world of stable, liberal and non-discriminatory trade policies is probably still more important for small, weak and trade-dependent economies than for the greater powers. It is just that the former can do little to bring it about.

What individual developing countries can do is position themselves to exploit the opportunities that will, one hopes, arise. But to achieve this goal they must first liberalize their trade policies. This, then, is the most important reason for examining impediments to trade liberalization in a number of developing countries.

Furthermore, trade liberalization by a number of developing countries would have an impact on the GATT system, even if undertaken outside that forum, provided it is associated with a rapid growth of their trade. The growth of exports (and imports) from Hong Kong, Singapore, the Republic of Korea and Taiwan shows that initially small economies can quite swiftly become important to the world economy. In fact, in 1984 the combined gross merchandise imports of these four trade-oriented developing economies was $109 billion, greater than those of Italy, France or the United Kingdom and seven times as much as those of either India or Brazil. (Indeed, *each* of the four imported far more than either of these latter countries.) In 1970, by contrast, the gross merchandise imports of the four developing economies had been less than $9 billion, almost exactly the same as those of Belgium at that time and about 40 per cent of those of the United Kingdom. Thus, the growth of the 'four little tigers', as they have sometimes been called, has been an important source of growth for world trade as a whole.[3]

Furthermore, successful trade liberalization by a large number of developing countries might lead to a change in the collective demands of developing countries. Up to now one of the most important goals of the developing countries has been that they remain free from most of the obligations of GATT membership and be allowed to pursue whatever protectionist trade policies they think appropriate. With widespread and successful liberalization, however, the demand could change and that, in turn, could make an important contribution to the viability of the system as a whole. In particular, developed countries might then feel somewhat less than they do now that liberalization is a cost borne by the rich for the beneit of the poor.

At the same time, membership of the GATT can offer some assistance to developing countries, when trying to liberalize. At present, the International Monetary Fund (IMF) and the World Bank are the main international institutions involved in helping developing countries with trade liberalization. In the case of the countries of Southern Europe agreements with the European Community play a major role in assisting liberalization. But, Mexico's accession to the GATT in 1986 indicates that membership can assist with liberalization by signalling the commitment to liberalize and making that commitment more credible.[4]

Furthermore, even if one were mainly concerned with the prospects for trade liberalization by countries now expected to participate more fully in the GATT system, one could not focus only on those cases, since they represent too limited a sample. Lessons have to be drawn from a wider sample.

Last but not least, the aim of participation in the GATT is trade liberalization. From this perspective, it dos not matter whether liberalization is achieved unilaterally or multilaterally. What matters is that it happens. It is necessary, therefore, to discover when and how liberalization is achieved.

Experience of the Philippines

The Philippines is the laggard in the world's most economically dynamic region. In each year between 1980 and 1985 the economies of each of the other South-east Asian developing countries grew faster than the Philippines. Moreover, the Philippines has the most severe debt problem of the region, one reminiscent of conditions in Latin American countries. Indeed, with a debt of $24 billion at the end of 1984 its debt to GDP ratio of 74 per cent compared most unfavourably with that of Argentina, at 60 per cent, of Brazil, at 56 per cent, and of Mexico, at 57 per cent.[5] Ultimately, this poor economic performance gravely undermined the government of Ferdinand Marcos and is the legacy with which that of Corazon Aquino must grapple.

As the study by Romeo Bautista demonstrates, these lamentable conditions are not new, though far worse than in previous decades. Relatively poor performance is long standing. Between 1965 and 1973 the GDP of the Philippines grew at 5.4 per cent a year and at 4.8 per cent between 1973 and 1984. These look to be satisfactory rates of growth, but not only did Hong Kong, the Republic of Korea and Singapore do far better in both periods, as one might anticipate, so did Indonesia, Malaysia and Thailand, countries with which the Philippines can more naturally be compared.[6] The economy of the Philippines has long been distorted by highly protectionist policies with a heavy bias against agriculture and exports of labour-intensive manufactures. These distortions have not only adversely affected economic performance, but have also been associated with a highly unequal distribution of income.

The protectionist policies of the Philippines can be dated to a foreign-exchange crisis in 1949-50. Protection then led to the usual temporary boom of import-substituting growth followed by increasingly chronic trade deficits at the end of the 1950s. The early 1960s saw the first tentative liberalization, but this was a modest effort. The combination of continued protection and ambitious development plans led to a renewed foreign-exchange crisis in late 1969.

A devaluation of the exchange rate in 1970 combined with a move to explicit export incentives to signal a shift to a more outward-looking development strategy. The effect of these reforms was to bring about a significant improvement of the incentive regime in just one important respect: a reduction in the bias against exports. Unfortunately, the improvement in the incentive to export was short-lived, there being a 30 per cent decline in the real exchange rate for exports between

1974 and 1979. Nevertheless, the improved incentive for exports was effective in raising the rate of growth of exports from 2.2 per cent in the 1960s to 7 per cent in the 1970s, growth of exports of non-traditional manufactures being particularly rapid. With improved export performance came higher growth of both agriculture and industry, although the effects on the distribution of income are ambiguous and uncertain.

In 1981, thc Philippincs embarked on an ambitious programme of trade liberalization, with the encouragement and assistance of the World Bank. The principal focus of this liberalization programme was tariff reform, although import licensing was also relaxed, at least for a while. Unfortunately, both the international and — still more — the domestic environments were most inauspicious for such a venture, which soon met its nemesis. The liberalization was swept away by the crisis of 1983, following the assassination of Benigno Aquino, when the economic and political chickens of the previous decade came home to roost.

On the economic front, after the first oil shock the Government of the Philippines had pursued expansionary fiscal and monetary policies financed by borrowing from abroad, the aim being to avoid adjustment to deteriorations in the terms of trade caused by the rise in the price of oil and declining commodity prices. These policies and the resulting substantial current account deficits persisted throughout the 1970s and early 1980s. The result was an appreciation of the real rate of exchange as the rate of nominal depreciation was slowed in the face of high domestic inflation. The effect was to offset the improved incentives for exports implicit in the devaluation of 1970, the impoved export incentives of the 1970s and the liberalization programme inaugurated in 1981. At the same time, the overvaluation of the real exchange rate encouraged private businessmen to borrow abroad and invest the proceeds in production for the highly protected home market, not a viable proposition in the long run. As long-term funds dried up from 1981, the first reaction was short-term borrowing, but as these funds dried up too, the government was forced to draw on reserves, which slumped to less than one month's imports by October 1983. In the face of the foreign exchange crisis the Government introduced stringent controls on foreign exchange and imports.

The crisis of 1983 had much in common with that of 1969. While an unfavourable external environment was an important cause of the problem, with the terms of trade declining some 40 per cent between 1972 and 1981-83, there was also the combination of risky, arguably reckless, macro-economic policy with a highly distorted structure of incentives. One of the consequences of those distortions was the persistent failure to expand exports at a satisfactory rate, such export expansion being perhaps the most important single determinant of creditworthiness.

Ideas, Interests and the Failure of Liberalization

As one would expect to be the case in an economy with a strongly protectionist tradition, exporters are simply too insignificant to exert appreciable influence over policy. In addition, many of the producers of export crops (especially coconuts and sugar) had invested in import substituting industries. Organized labour had neither much infuence on the government of Ferdinand Marcos nor a clear position on the desirability of liberalization. A large part of the business class was, quite naturally, strongly opposed to liberalization and, in a regime like that of President Marcos, their objections were like to carry substantial weight. Finally, large and important elements of the bureaucracy were, again for evident reasons of self-interest, strongly opposed to liberalization.

The move of the Philippines towards export promotion in the 1970s and again towards liberalization in the early 1980s reflected in large measure the intellectual convictions of a group of Western educated and influenced technocrats who held important positions in the government. Prominent among them were Gerardo Sicat, Chairman of the National Economic

Council from 1970 and subsequently Minister of Economic Planning from 1974 to 1981 and Cesar Virata, Prime Minister during the liberalization of the early 1980s. These technocrats had become well aware of the pervasive distortions in the structure of incentives and the unfavourable performance of the economy relative to its immediate neighbours. By this time nobody in that part of the world could be unaware of the importance of having an efficient trade policy regime, especially one with neutrality between the incentives for production for foreign and domestic markets. In the case of the liberalization of the 1980s there was also the pressure exerted by the World Bank's new structural adjustment lending. In all, the attempts at liberalization represent as clear an example as one would wish of the fight of ideas against protectionist interests.

The opposition to the liberalization programme of the early 1980s was significant and won a number of victories. Nevertheless, the programme is judged by Dr Bautista to have been the most significant attempted in the Philippines. The combination of the perceived gains from export expansion with the offer of World Bank money was quite persuasive. In the end, the foreign-exchange crisis of 1983 swept it away, as foreign private lending dried up. The economy contracted by 10 per cent in the following two years and the resulting distress was an important contributory cause of the collapse of the Marcos regime in 1986. It was the fiscal crisis of the state, therefore, more than the detailed opposition of vested interests to individual parts of the programme, that ensured that hasty retreat from liberalization.

Role of International Support for Reform

In the Philippines, as in other developing countries with long histories of protectionism and failed attempts at liberalization, there are those who argue that the present unfavourable international economic environment undermines the case for outward-looking policies. Painful change, it is suggested (with a sigh of relief), is unnecessary. Dr Bautista gives short shrift to these arguments, noting that an adverse international environment 'does not imply that the efficiency with which domestic resources are being used no longer matters'. Indeed, one might suggest that it matters more. As the study notes, it is impossible for the Philippines to dispense with trade. Accordingly, the country can also not dispense with the need to earn and save foreign exchange efficiently, this being the principal purpose of trade policy. Efficient use of resources may be a luxury in a world of bouyant trade and growth, since almost everyone can succeed. In a hostile environment, however, efficiency is a necessity since the difference between it and its obverse may be that between advance and decline in income per capita, especially when the population is expected to grow at over 2 per cent a year.[7]

Nevertheless, the external environment determines the level of performance to be expected after policy reform. Dr Bautista notes that the Philippines has been gravely damaged by the two most significant components of developed-country protectionism, in agriculture and in textiles and clothing. The country could also benefit from liberalization by other developing countries, especially newly industrializing countries like the Republic of Korea and Taiwan.

As is true of many developing countries, the Philippines sees the GATT as unable to protect its trading interests, especially given (i) the growth of discriminatory protection, (ii) the increasing number of bilateral deals between the United States, Japan and the European Community, (iii) the growing distortions in world trade in agriculture, and (iv) the persistent resistance to imports of labour-intensive manufactures (especially clothing) from so-called 'low cost' producers. Naturally enough, developing countries like the Philippines tend to regard calls from the developed countries for greater compliance with the GATT as blatant hypocrisy.

The World Bank and the IMF are, at present, more significant players than the GATT in the drama of the Philippines. On the whole, Dr Bautista is content with the general direction of World Bank pressure for liberalization, but is concerned about the stance of the IMF. There is a danger that an undue emphasis on demand restriction rather than on improved incentives, including a substantial real devaluation, will not only impair immediate economic performance but damage it in the longer term because of a decline in investment and a squeeze on essential imports of inputs for exports. If the Philippines is to succeed, a radical programme to improve the efficiency of resource use and to control public finance must be combined with continued inflows of resources from abroad (especially debt relief). As Dr Bautista notes, 'the more restrictive are the required adjustment policies, the greater is the risk of further aggravating political instability and the chances that the IMF performance criteria and debt service obligations will not be met.'

Lessons from the Philippines Experience

In many ways the case of the Philippines is tragic. Blessed with a favourable resource endowment and located in the world's most economically dynamic region, her economy has lagged behind those of her neighbours and in the 1980s the country has suffered an economic and political crisis of Latin American proportions. These economic and political crises are in no way independent, with a corrupt political system encouraging both protection and excessive fiscal expansion and with poor economic performance, in turn, impairing the legitimacy of the political regime and so encouraging even more protection and fiscal profligacy in the ultimately futile attempt to buy domestic support. The ability of the Government of the Philippines to borrow abroad following the first oil shock made this fundamentally unsustainable set of policies feasible for almost a decade, but a huge build-up of debt (which also became increasingly short term) rendered the Philippines acutely vulnerable to the change in the sentiment of lenders that happened in the early 1980s.

In the Philippines, attempts have been made about once a decade to improve trade policy, most notably in the increase export orientation of the early 1970s and the trade liberalization programme of the early 1980s. In both cases macro-economic imbalances undermined the attempt at micro-economic reform. In this crucial respect the case of the Philippines appears to be representative of that of many developing countries. The capacity of interest groups to undermine the stability of the public finances appears to be more fatal for liberalism in trade policy than their direct efforts to obtain protection or resist liberalization. Certainly, the two together appear to render liberalization virtually impossible.

Potection that has been in effect for more than a generation permeates the body politic like a cancer. The bureaucracy and much of the political class live by handing out the lucrative favours from which businessmen grow rich. The market that matters to businessmen is then the political market. The associated corruption of the political process may itself contribute to the fiscal problems that first cause protection and then undermine liberalization. In such an unfavourable context boldness and determination are needed to bring results and these qualities are only likely to appear when the previous political and economic regime has collapsed. The fact that such a collapse has occurred gives the Philippines a special opportunity. Since experience suggsts that attempts to exploit such opportunities are rarely successful, the Philippines needs every assistance from international institutions and governments of major countries. Both the Government of the Philippines and potential supporters need to remember that this is an opportunity that will not long endure.

NOTES AND REFERENCES

1. T.G. Congdon, *Economic Liberalism in the Cone of Latin America*, Thames Essay No. 40 (London: Trade Policy Research Centre, 1985).

2. The author has discussed the influence of GATT agreements on developing countries and of individual developing countries on agrements in the GATT in 'Two-Edged Sword: Demands of Development Countries and the Trading System', in Jagdish N.

Bhagwati and John Gerard Ruggie (eds), *Power, Passions and Purpose: Prospects for North-South Negotiations* (Cambridge, Massachusetts: MIT Press, 1984) and Martin Wolf 'Differential and More Favourable Treatment of Developing Countries and the International Trading System', mimeograph (1986). Paper prepared for the Conference on the Role and Interests of the Developing Countries in the Multilateral Trade Negotiations, sponsored by the World Bank and the Thailand Development Research Institute, Bangkok, 30 October to 1 November 1986.

3. Data on imports in 1984 are from *World Development Report 1986* (New York: Oxford University Press, for the World Bank, 1986) Annex Table 9 and *Financial Statistics: Taiwan District, the Republic of China,* February 1987, Taipei, Central Bank of China. Data on imports for 1970s are from *International Financial Statistics Yearbook 1986*, International Monetary Fund, Washington, and *World Tables 1976* (Baltimore and London: Johns Hopkins Press, for the World Bank,1976).

4. On the role of outside institutions in liberalization, see Wolf, 'Timing and Sequencing of Trade Liberalization', *Asian Development Reveiw*, Vol. 4, No. 2, 1986, pp. 1-24.

5. Data on indebtedness are from *World Development Report 1986*, *op. cit.*, Annex Tables 3 and 15.

6. Data on economic growth are from *World Development Report 1986*, *op. cit.*, Annex Table 2.

7. Data on population growth are from *World Development Report 1986*, *op. cit.*, Annex Table 25.

Chapter 1

Introduction and Overview of the Economy

SINCE the beginning of the 1980s the growth of the Philippine economy has slowed markedly relative to both the country's past economic performance during the post-World War II period and the contemporaneous record of other market economies in the East Asian region. The continuous decline in the growth rate of the real gross national product (GNP) from 6.7 per cent in 1979 to 4.7 per cent in 1980, 3.6 per cent in 1981, 2.8 per cent in 1982, and 1.4 per cent in 1983 was without precedent in the post-war economic history of the Philippines. Over the same period the country's annual current account deficit reached record high levels, averaging US$2.4 billion or about 46 per cent of total exports. Commonly cited as the underlying reasons are the sluggish growth of the economies of industrialized countries since 1980, the intensification of protectionism in the markets of those countries (particularly against labour-intensive manufactures), and the steep fall in world commodity prices. But the same factors would have impeded economic growth in neighbouring Asian countries which, however, did not seem to have been affected so severely.[1]

The Philippine situation turned from bad to worse in the wake of the assassination of leading opposition politician Benigno Aquino in August 1983. The resultant political turmoil induced a massive flight of capital and a drastic reduction in foreign loans, exposing the fragility of the country's balance of payments and external debt position.

Total debt outstanding at the end of 1983 was about $26 billion, of which about 40 per cent was short term. A liquidity crisis soon developed as foreign bank lenders refused to 'roll over' these short-term debts, a practice which had been taken for granted previously in more favourable circumstances. A moratorium on repayment of debt principal took effect on 17 October 1983 and, after a lengthy process of negotiation, the International Monetary Fund (IMF) gave approval to a $615 million special drawing rights (SDRs) standby credit for the Philippines that would pave the way for debt rescheduling and new borrowing from foreign banks. In exchange, the Marcos Government promised to reduce the country's budget deficit and money supply growth, among other conditions.

As the foreign exchange crisis took its toll and contractionary policy measures were adopted, there was an absolute decline in real GNP by about 10 per cent in 1984-85. Thus, when Corazon Aquino assumed power in February 1986, the country's per capita income in real terms was down to the 1975 level, existing production capacity was severely under-utilized and massive unemployment and under-employment existed.

Given these circumstances and the over-riding concern of Philippine economic policy makers with debt-servicing and stabilization problems, any discussion of trade liberalization issues and suggestions for liberalizing the trade regime may seem quite inopportune. This is, however, a very short-term and superficial view. An orderly repayment of debt can be facilitated by an improvement in a country's general economic performance and trade liberalization is an important means of achieving this goal. There are, of course, other elements of Philippine economic policy that need to be reformed (and they will not be ignored in the following discussion) but trade-related policies seem to present the critical dimension in a policy mixture that would provide a basis for future stable growth of the Philippine economy.

To understand why and how trade liberalization can make a significant difference to the future economic performance of the Philippines, it is necessary to go back into the past and see how the country's post-World War II economic record has been affected by the foreign trade and payments policies adopted. This is done in Chapter 2 of this essay. The recurrence of balance-of-payments crises is shown to be related to the highly protective and distorted trade policies which were adopted throughout most of the post-war period. There had been a significant improvement in the general policy climate for export expansion in the early 1970s which, however, was not sustained through the rest of the decade. Instead, the government expanded its market intervention activities in response to external shocks during the middle and later 1970s; also, selective promotion of export industries was resorted to although the pervasive bias against exporting remained in the country's incentive system. Nevertheless, the increased outward orientation must have contributed to the improved performance of the Philippine economy in the 1970s relative to the two previous decades.

By the late 1970s Philippine policy makers were acutely aware of the need to improve further the international competitiveness of domestic industry which, in comparison with other market economies in South-east Asia, was more heavily protected from foreign competition.[2] A programme of 'industrial structural adjustment' was initiated in 1981, with technical and financial support from the World Bank, including trade liberalization measures more comprehensive than those adopted earlier. In Chapter 3 of this essay an assessment is made of the programme and other policy developments which accompanied this trade liberalization effort are discussed. Although it was overtaken by the foreign-exchange and debt-servicing problems which began in August 1983, it is instructive to examine the various components of the programme and how other aspects of policy impinged on the trade liberalization measures. This will then provide a basis for developing suggestions for the formulation and implementation of future trade liberalization policies.

As far as the conduct of macro-economic policies is

concerned, it seems reasonable to state that a serious miscalculation was made in responding to unfavourable developments in the international economic environment in the early 1980s. In opting for what was touted as a 'counter-cyclical' expansionary fiscal and monetary policy, Philippine policy makers failed to anticipate the severity of the resulting trade deficits, which were exacerbated by the sharply deteriorating terms of trade. While some accommodation was made possible, initially, by heavy external borrowing, it quickly led to a situation where additional borrowing was needed simply to service the outstanding debt. Political factors undoubtedly precipitated the crisis; but the inability to cope with the current account deficits and sustain the high growth strategy was basically due to the highly protective and distorted trade and industrial policies that prevented the achievement of a commensurate expansion of exports and efficient domestic investment.

In Chapter 4 the discussion shifts to some aspects of the political economy of Philippine trade policies. Although there had been previous attempts at trade liberalization, none was more comprehensive and significant than that which accompanied the industrial structural adjustment programme initiated in 1981. This was made possible by a commitment at the highest policy level to a liberalization of the trade regime which, in turn, was influenced by the availability of financial and technical assistance from the World Bank at a time of need. The increased political leverage of the World Bank and the IMF in the post-crisis period would seem to imply that firm guidance will continue to be provided by these two organizations in Philippine policy making, especially in the direction of structural adjustment and eventual trade liberalization. The possibility cannot be ruled out, however, that over-strict 'performance criteria' could generate domestic political pressures that may result in less government commitment to needed policy reforms.

The international aspects of trade liberalization are more comprehensively discussed in Chapter 5. Although a liberalized foreign trade regime is desirable regardless of what may happen in the external sector, it would certainly help the country's trade performance if foreign demand for its exports were to rise through a sustained economic recovery and a retreat from protectionism in the markets of developed countries. The Philippines can also benefit from trade liberalization among the Asian newly-industrializing countries (NICs), especially for imports of labour-intensive manufactures and resource-based products. As the comparative advantage of the NICs shifts to more sophisticated industrial products, import demand for labour-intensive manufactures will increase in their own domestic markets. If there is a significant reduction in trade barriers in the NICs, the 'near-NICs', including the Philippines, can be expected to expand their exports of such products while increasing their imports of machinery and other producer goods from the NICs. Improvements in the external economic environment can help overcome domestic resistance to trade liberalization.

In the Philippine context the need for improved access to foreign markets is heightened by the debt service problem, the severity of which will depend on such external factors as movements in the country's terms of trade, the behaviour of interest rates and terms of debt repayments (still to be negotiated with foreign bank creditors). International organizations such as the General Agreement on Tariffs and Trade (GATT), the IMF, and the World Bank can help by working to improve the conditions of world trade and payments. Political leverage by these organizations, especially the IMF, can also be used to persuade foreign bank lenders to agree to lighten the burden for debtor less developed countries (LDCs) through concessionary repayment terms. The setting of IMF stabilization policy targets and performance criteria also need to be realistic and flexible in the face of exogenous shocks to the domestic economy outside the control of policy makers.

The final chapter offers some concluding comments about the prospects for trade liberalization in the Philippines under the Aquino Government and suggests how other policies can help to improve micro-economic efficiency and establish a basis for future stable growth of the Philippine economy. Various impediments which could inhibit the policy changes necessary to bring about a more open trade regime are recognized. Excessive expenditure reduction, as required in the conditions laid down by the IMF, together with stringent debt repayment terms, could have adverse repercussions on output and employment that may create additional political pressures and weaken the government's commitment to policy reforms.

Export expansion, which stimulates growth, is a more efficient instrument for balance-of-payments adjustment than the compression of imports, which inhibits growth. To be able to pursue the former strategy in reducing the gap between domestic expenditure and domestic output over time, the Philippines needs to have continued access to export markets and adequate inflows of foreign resources. In turn, Philippine policy makers should exercise fiscal and financial prudence to achieve macro-economic stabilization, as well as implementing trade liberalization and other policy measures to improve the overall efficiency of the economy.

NOTES AND REFERENCES

1. Thus, each of the other South-east Asian countries performed better, in terms of the growth of real GNP, than the Philippines in each year from 1980 to 1985.

2. *Tariff Profiles in ASEAN* (Manila: National Economic and Development Authority, for the Tariff Commission, 1979).

Chapter 2

Domestic Policies and the Structure of Protection

PHILIPPINE economic development in the post-World War II period has been significantly influenced by the trade and payments policies adopted and their effects on sectoral production incentives. Other economic policies have generally tended to reinforce those effects.

Import Substitution in the 1950s and 1960s

As an *ad hoc* response to a severe balance-of-payments problem, controls on imports and foreign exchange were instituted in 1949-50. Together with a heavily over-valued domestic currency (the pre-war exchange rate of two pesos per United States dollar had been retained) the criterion of 'essentiality' governed the system of trade controls. This created a strong bias towards domestic production of substitutes for finished industrial consumer goods, imports of which were not considered to be essential. Imported raw materials, intermediate products, and capital goods, on the other hand, were obtained at artificially low prices (in peso terms). This effectively penalized the primary producing sectors (agriculture and mining), export-oriented industries, and intermediate and capital goods production (categories which are, of course, not mutually exclusive). The chronic trade deficits witnessed in the 1950s, particularly during the second half of the decade, were a reflection of the increasing dependence of domestic industries on imports and the inability to stimulate new exports.

Towards the end of the 1950s there was little room left for 'non-essential' imports, as imports of producer goods already amounted to nearly 90 per cent of the annual import bill. The worsening trade deficit prompted the authorities gradually to dismantle the control system and to rationalize the foreign exchange rate. The lifting of import and foreign exchange controls and currency devaluation (to 3.9 pesos per United States dollar) in the early 1960s represented the country's first episode of trade liberalization. The policy reforms, however, did not alter very much the incentive structure favouring consumer goods industries producing import substitutes. A highly protective tariff system, introduced in 1957, but made redundant at that time by the import and foreign exchange controls, preserved the character of a protective structure which was biased against exports and backward integration.[1]

The 1960s were consequently attended also by balance-of-payments difficulties, accentuated in the second half of the decade by the expansionary monetary and fiscal policies that the government (of the newly-elected President Ferdinand Marcos) adopted. According to Robert E. Baldwin, of the University of Wisconsin,

> '...in addition to providing easier credit conditions, the new Administration embarked upon a large-scale programme of economic development ... in order to finance capital formation activities of the national and local governments, as well as those of such government corporations as the Development Bank of the Philippines, and also provide funds for expanded current expenditures on development services, it was necessary for the government to engage in extensive borrowing, both internally and externally.'[2]

Accordingly, from 1965 to 1969 both the internal and external public debt nearly doubled.

In late 1969 a foreign exchange crisis developed, precipitated by the need to service short-term credit that had financed the trade deficits of the immediately preceding years. The policy response was to float the Philippine peso in February 1970 and eliminate some of the exchange controls which had been operative since 1967. By December 1970 the exchange rate had settled at 6.4 pesos per United States dollar, representing an effective devaluaton of 61.4 per cent over the year.

Export Promotion in the 1970s

This *de facto* peso devaluation was followed by the enactment of the Export Incentives Act of 1970, signalling a policy shift towards a more outward-looking strategy of industrial development and away from the heavy import-substitution drive of the previous two decades. Both measures recognized the need to orient local industries more towards the export market and to expand non-traditional exports. Among other incentives, manufacturing firms registered with the Board of Investments (BOI) under the Export Incentives Act qualified for various kinds of tax exemptions, deductions from taxable income, and tax credits.

In addition to the improved exchange rate and fiscal incentives, export producers also received, on a selective basis, various forms of financial and infrastructure support, serving to compensate, in part, for the still pervasive bias against exporting in the country's incentive system. The highly protective and distorted tariff system was the primary source of this bias but no attempt was made to deal directly with either the protection or the distortion in the tariff system as part of the export promotion programme during the 1970s.[3]

Exogenous Shocks and Policy Responses

The decade of the 1970s was a period of relative instability for the Philippine economy, because of both internal and external disturbances.[4] The social unrest which began in late 1970 led to the declaration of martial law by President Marcos in September 1972. This was to have a significant influence on the nature of the policy reactions to the exogenous shocks coming from the external sector.

In response to the external shocks the government assumed an increasing role in the regulation of, and direct participation in, production and marketing activities which the broad powers of the martial law regime facilitated. The oil crisis of 1973-74 revealed the government's lack of control over one of the most strategic sectors of the economy. The government has since taken a substantial direct role in the import of crude oil and in the refining and distribution of petroleum products, reducing significantly the dominance of foreign oil companies.

Agriculture was also subject to government intervention in the 1970s to a degree and scope which was unparalleled in previous decades. The intervention was ostensibly aimed at shielding the sector from the pronounced instability of the external economic environment. A government monopoly of external trade in the staple foodgrains (rice, corn and wheat) was the primary means of regulating their domestic price levels. It was supplemented by direct price controls which in the 1970s tended to lower the domestic prices of food crops relative to world prices. Trade in coconut and sugar — the country's dominant export crops — was particularly subject to government regulation from the early 1970s. An export quota for sugar was in operation from 1962 and from 1970, sugar trading in both domestic and foreign markets was taken over by state corporations. In the case of coconuts, a production tax was introduced in 1973 at rates averaging about 20 per cent of the border price of copra. From 1970 a 6 per cent export tax was also levied on copra and sugar; other agricultural exports were taxed at rates ranging from 4-10 per cent. In addition, export premium duties on agricultural products were imposed in 1973, which served partly to siphon off the gains from the world commodity boom at the time.

Effects on the Incentive Structure

These policy measures had the effect of artificially depressing the domestic prices of agricultural products. Nominal protection rates, representing the excess of the domestic price of a product over its international price, were estimated to be minus 6.1 per cent and minus 15.9 per cent on average for food and export crops, respectively, in the 1970s.[5]

Indeed, apart from poultry, meat and eggs, negative protection rates have generally characterized all agricultural products.

To some extent, also, government intervention in agricultural input markets has reinforced the policy bias against agricultural production. Except for irrigation subsidies,[6] government policies have tended to raise the domestic prices of agricultural inputs relative to their social opportunity costs. Estimated implicit tariff rates, indicating the excess of the domestic price of an input over its border price, for the 1970s were 10 per cent for fertilizer, 23 per cent for other agricultural chemicals, 10 per cent for four-wheeled tractors, 33 per cent for hand tractors, and 30 per cent for irrigation pumps.[7]

As a measure of relative incentives, effective protection rates (EPRs) — or rates of protection of value added by domestic factors, representing the proportionate difference between domestic and foreign value added — are more meaningful than nominal protection and implicit tariff rates. This is because EPRs include both the subsidy to domestic producers from the protection of outputs and the penalty from the protection of inputs. A study of effective protection in the Philippines, based on tariffs and indirect taxes in the mid-1970s, showed the weighted average EPR for manufacturing industries to be 44 per cent compared to only 9 per cent for the primary sectors (agriculture and mining).[8] Export-oriented sectors had an EPR of 4 per cent compared to 61 per cent for non-exporting industries. The other findings of this study, together with the EPR estimates in earlier studies for 1965 and for 1949-71, indicate the persistence of a strong bias in the tariff structure and the indirect tax system in favour of consumer goods at the expense of intermediate products and capital goods.

The effective subsidy arising from the fiscal incentives accorded to BOI-registered export producers has been observed to be relatively large for *firms* that actually availed themselves of the tax benefits but for BOI-subsidized *industries*, the average EPR in 1974 appears to have risen by only about 5 per cent. This reflects the inability of many firms, particularly the smaller, to gain access to BOI export incentives.

The effect of exchange rate policy on the relative profitability of export production can be represented by the 'purchasing power parity-effective exchange rate' (PPP-EER for short) using Professor Baldwin's terminology. This is obtained by multiplying the 'effective exchange rate' (representing the number of units of local currency per dollar actually received by exporters) by the export unit value index and dividing by the general wholesale price index. The PPP-EER estimates for 1970-71 were found by Robert Baldwin to have increased by 40 per cent for traditional exports and by 65 per cent for non-traditional exports from the corresponding average PPP-EERs during 1967-69.[9] There can be no doubt, therefore, that the policy measures adopted in the early 1970s had considerably enhanced the attractiveness of production for export *vis-á-vis* domestic sales.

After 1974, however, the PPP-EER of the peso declined significantly and in 1979 it was lower by about 30 per cent compared to the 1974 value. This would seem to indicate that exchange rate policy and aggregate demand management 'had not been successfully utilized during the second half of the decade, in the light of the exogenous export price movements, to sustain the real devaluation achieved earlier'.[10]

Effects on Sectoral Production and Exports

The consequence of import-substitution policies for Philippine industrial growth was favourable during the first half of the 1950s: value added in manufacturing increased by an average of 15.8 per cent from 1949 to 1956. After this exuberant stage associated with the sudden increase in the private profitability of some industrial investments, however, opportunities for production of consumer goods began to decline because of the limited size of the domestic market. There was a sharp deceleration in the growth of manufacturing production to 6.3 per cent annually during the period 1956-60, followed by a moderate rise to 6.7 per cent in the 1960s.

As the policy climate for export expansion generally

improved, industrial production picked up further, achieving a 7.2 per cent average annual rate of increase during the 1970s. This was due, in part, to the remarkable expansion of non-traditional manufactured exports, which grew at an unprecedented rate of about 20 per cent annually in volume terms. These new industrial exports consisted mostly of labour-intensive manufactured products such as garments, electronic products, furniture, other wood products, and so on.

Heavy protection of domestic industry has, however, retarded the growth not only of manufacturing but also of agricultural production and exports, since the over-valuation of the Philippine peso, made possible by industrial import restrictions, acted as a tax on agricultural exports. The annual growth rate of agricultural value added was only about 3.8 per cent from the mid-1950s to the late 1960s; it increased to 4.5 per cent in the 1970s. The acceleration of agricultural growth in the 1970s was fuelled by a rapid expansion and diversification of agricultural exports, paralleling the country's industrial export performance over the same period. Coconut and sugar-cane products, which used to account for more than 70 per cent of total Philippine export earnings, were contributing only 55 per cent by the late 1970s as bananas, pineapples, shrimps, tuna, coffee and other non-traditional agricultural exports assumed greater shares.

Even in the 1970s, though, three sources of domestic price distortions effectively penalized agricultural activities, namely, the under-pricing of food, the taxation of agricultural exports and the under-valuation of foreign exchange. It has been estimated that the correction of these three policy biases, that is, a complete liberalization of agricultural pricing and exchange rate policies, could have led to an increase in agricultural crop income in the Philippines by as much as 30 per cent.[11]

Macro-economic Effects

The growth of total exports, in volume terms, averaged 7 per cent annually during 1970-80. This figure is significantly higher than the 2.2 per cent growth registered in the preceding decade, which is not surprising given the observed shift toward more outward-looking policies initiated in the early 1970s. A similar, if less dramatic, increase also took place in the growth rate of GNP in the 1970s; it averaged 6.2 per cent annually compared to 5.1 per cent in the 1960s. While these comparative statistics do not, on their own, establish the superiority of outward-oriented over inward-oriented development policies, they are consistent with the well-established empirical association between 'superior export performance' and 'superior economic performance' among developing countries (at least in terms of the growth rate of real national income).[12] It should also be noted that the above improvements in the export and output performance of the Philippine economy occurred at a time of increased instability in the world economy (relative to the 1950s and 1960s) and rising protectionism in the markets of developed countries.

Because employment and income distribution problems are major concerns of development policy in the Philippines, it is important to examine whether the policy shifts towards a more outward-oriented development tended to have positive effects on employment generation and on the narrowing of income disparities. Increased production for export of labour-intensive manufactures and of more highly processed primary products were especially favoured by the new policies, so there is a presumptive case that they will lead to greater industrial labour absorption. This is, however, not borne out by the available employment data which indicate that the contribution of manufacturing to total employment in the Philippines remained roughly constant, at about 12 per cent, from the mid-1950s to the late 1970s.

Such a result would not be surprising in the period prior to 1970, during which time industrial and trade policies led to a structure of incentives biased toward the use of capital. During the period of foreign exchange and import controls in the 1950s, the 'essentiality' rule conferred private benefits on the import of capital equipment. With 'decontrol' in the 1960s, the low tariff rates on imported machinery and equipment had much the same effect, discriminating against labour use. Indeed, there is empirical evidence that the industries which used relatively more labour had lower rates of export growth during the period from 1954 to 1969.[13]

But what would explain the apparent paradox of rapidly expanding exports of labour-intensive manufactures in the 1970s with no discernible increase in the share of the manufacturing sector in overall employment? One possibility would be that, despite the rapid growth, the very small base of labour-intensive industrial exports at the start of the period precluded a measurable employment effect. Another explanation is that, even in the 1970s, relative factor pricing was biased against labour use: the fiscal incentives given to BOI-registered enterprises have been shown in previous studies to have a capital-cheapening effect. Lastly, and this may well provide the 'best' explanation, the general improvement in the policy climate induced an economy-wide generation of employment opportunities, so that increases in manufacturing employment were matched in the rest of the economy. Aggregate measures of unemployment and under-employment provide some support for the foregoing explanation. Based on published statistics, open unemployment in the 1970s (ranging from 3.9 to 5.2 per cent of the labour force) was much lower than in the 1950s and 1960s (above 7 per cent). Similarly, under-employment rates appear to have decreased from about 21-22 per cent in the early 1960s to 11 per cent in 1975. It should be pointed out, however, that the problem of interpreting trends in Philippine employment statistics is considerable in view of frequent changes in the coverage and timing of household surveys.[14]

The effect on income distribution of the increased export orientation of the Philippine economy in the 1970s is also difficult to document, again owing to problems related to data reliability. On theoretical grounds, an improvement would be expected in real rewards to the abundant factors, labour and natural resources; this might have raised the income shares of wage earners and rural workers. It is not easy, however, to translate this into the effects on the distribution of income or on the income of poor families. Available official statistics indicate that the Gini coefficient (indicating the degree of inequality) remained at around 0.50 from 1956 to 1971, but had declined to 0.44 by 1975. However, the results of the 1975 Family Income and Expenditure Survey, on which the latter finding is based, have been challenged and an alternative estimate of the Gini coefficient for 1975, placed at 0.51, implied no reduction in income inequality in the first half of the 1970s.[15]

It seems reasonable to state, therefore, that factors other than the policy shifts toward export promotion had affected income distribution in the Philippines more significantly. For one thing, the dramatic developments in the world economy in the 1970s produced wide swings in the country's terms of trade which tended to raise or to lower sharply the income share of rural households. This highlighted the marked disparity in urban and rural incomes in the Philippines and the heavy dependence of rural income on commodity export earnings. On this basis it may not be far-fetched to hypothesize that there was an improvement in income distribution during the first half of the 1970s, spurred by the commodity boom of 1972-74, but that the subsequent collapse of primary product export prices had adverse equity effects in the second half of the 1970s.

Real wage changes would be another determinant of income distribution in the Philippines, since common labourers are at the bottom end of the income scale. Some analysts have alluded to the deterioration of real wage rates in the 1970s as an indication of increasing income inequality, the blame being placed on the 'various restrictions on the workers' right to strike and to self-organization' since the declaration of martial law.[16] Based on Central Bank data for metropolitan Manila, real wage rates appear to have declined not only in the 1970s but, indeed, since the mid-1950s.[17] When 1972 is used as the base year the index shows a decreasing trend from 142 in 1955 to 133 in 1960, 115 in 1965, 76 in 1974, and 71 in 1979. This wage index, however, is for basic wage rates and does not include the wage supplements in the form of cost-of-living allowances, 13-month pay, *et cetera*, periodically decreed since 1974. On the assumption that these supplementary wage earnings were fully implemented, the 'true' real wage rate index would have reversed its downward trend by 1976, climbing to 128 in 1980. Unfortunately, it is not possible to ascertain from available statistics the degree to which the wage supplements were actually granted by private employers.

To return to trade issues, it may appear surprising that substantial current account deficits persisted in the 1970s, despite the marked expansion and diversification of Philippine exports. This is due, in part, to adverse movements in the terms of trade especially in the aftermath of the 1973-74 oil price shock which, during 1975-77, was accompanied by steep declines in commodity export prices. Another reason is that Philippine policy makers opted for growth and were unwilling to curtail imports of producer goods. As will be seen in the next chapter, the trade deficits were mainly financed by foreign borrowing, thus avoiding any significant depreciation of the domestic currency at that time. Lastly, there was a continuing reliance on imported intermediate inputs, related presumably to the failure to correct existing policy biases against backward linkage. While the penalties to export production were partially compensated for by fiscal and financial incentives as well as infrastructure support, there were no corresponding offsets toward the promotion of backward integration. A superior strategy, of course, would have been to eliminate directly the sources of those policy biases.

NOTES AND REFERENCES

1. This was pointed out in the first systematic analysis of post-war trade policies in the Philippines and their effects on relative incentives, resource allocation, and industrial development; see John

H. Power and Gerardo P. Sicat, *The Philippines: Industrialisation and Trade Policies* (London: Oxford University Press, 1971). Backward integration refers to the use of domestically produced inputs into final production.

2. Robert E. Baldwin, *Foreign Trade Regimes and Economic Development: The Philippines* (New York: National Bureau of Economic Research, 1975) pp. 66-67.

3. The Revised Tariff Code of 1973 simplified the structure of rates, and actually raised more duties than it lowered.

4. For a detailed discussion, see Romeo M. Bautista, 'Structural Change in the Philippines' in Lawrence B. Krause and Sueo Sekiguchi (eds), *Economic Interaction in the Pacific Basin* (Washington: Brookings Institution, 1980).

5. Bautista, 'Domestic Price Distortions and Agricultural Income in Developing Countries', *Journal of Development Economics*, Amsterdam, Vol. XXIII, No. 1, 1986, pp. 19-39.

6. For gravity irrigation, the most common system used in the Philippines, collected fees amount to only about 14 per cent of the annualized cost of irrigation per hectare.

7. Cristina C. David, 'Economic Policies and Philippine Agriculture', paper presented at the workshop on the Impact of Economic Policies on Agricultural Development sponsored by the Philippine Institute for Development Studies in Tagaytay City, 25-26 June 1983.

8. Norma A. Tan, 'The Structure of Protection and Resource Flows in the Philippines', in Bautista, Power and Associates, *Industrial Promotion Policies in the Philippines* (Manila: Philippine Institute for Development Studies, 1979).

9. Baldwin, *op. cit.*, pp. 90-91.

10. Bautista, 'Industrial Growth and Structural Adjustment in the Philippines', paper presented at the Conference on Patterns of Growth and Structural Change in Asia's NICs and Near-NICs in the Context of Economic Interdependence, sponsored by the East-West Center in Honolulu, 3-9 April 1983, p. 7.

11. See Bautista, 'Domestic Price Distortions and Agricultural Income in Developing Countries', *loc. cit.*

12. Jagdish N. Bhagwati and T.N. Srinivasan, 'Trade Policy and Development' in Rudiger Dornbusch and Jacob Frenkel (eds), *International Economic Policy: Theory and Evidence* (Baltimore: Johns Hopkins Press, 1978).

13. Bautista, 'Employment Effects of Export Expansion in the

Philippines', *Malayan Economic Review*, Kuala Lumpur, April 1975.

14. For a comprehensive assessment of official employment statistics, see Rosalinda P. Tidalgo and Emmanuel F. Esguerra, *Philippine Employment in the Seventies* (Manila: Philippine Institute for Development Studies, 1984).

15. See Mahar Mangahas and Bruno Barros, *The Distribution of Income and Wealth: a Survey of Philippine Research*, School of Economics Discussion Paper 7916 (Manila: University of the Philippines, 1979).

16. Gonzalo M. Jurado, Ricardo D. Ferrer and Emmanuel F. Esguerra, 'Trade Policy, Growth and Employment: A Study of the Philippines', paper prepared for the International Labour Office, Geneva, 1983.

17. On this basis, and also because of the 'enormous windfall gains and profit opportunities in the industrial sector ... exploited by the vigorous entrepreneurial group', Professor Baldwin has concluded that 'the major beneficiaries of the government's development policies (in the 1950s and 1960s) have been those who run or control businesses in the industrial sector'; see Baldwin, *op. cit.*, p. 149.

Chapter 3

Economic Aspects of the Trade Liberalization Programme

IT WOULD BE helpful at this stage to examine the attempt at trade liberalization which was part of a wider programme of policy reforms and industrial restructuring started in 1981. Although policy actions dealing with short-term contingencies related to the later foreign exchange crisis superseded some of the components of the programme, it constitutes a point of departure from which to examine the liberalization efforts of the Marcos Government. Related developments in other policy areas leading to the 1983 foreign exchange crisis are also discussed in this chapter.

Tariff Policy and Import Licensing

Tariffs form one of the areas of major policy reform; this component of the trade liberalization programme was not much prejudiced by short-term policy considerations. Peak tariff rates of 70 to 100 per cent were reduced to 50 per cent in two stages on 1 Janaury 1981 and 1 January 1982. Very low tariff rates, on the other hand, were raised to at least 10 per cent by 1985. Based on the overall tariff changes scheduled for the period 1981-85, the average tariff rate should have declined from 43 per cent in 1980 to 28 per cent by 1985. Moreover, the degree of dispersion should also have been lower by 1985.

Analysis of the effects of the tariff reform made by the author indicates substantial tariff liberalization by 1985, in terms of both the overall reduction in effective protection and the narrowing of the EPR disparities among manufacturing industries (Table 3.1). If the end-use category classification is used it can be shown that consumer goods industries continued to enjoy the highest tariff protection, even after the very substantial decline in average effective protection rates for those industries from 115 per cent in 1980 to 43 per cent in 1985.[1] Intermediate and capital goods sectors, on the other hand, which in 1980 were already being accorded relatively lower tariff protection (compared to consumer goods production) also faced a reduction in effective rates,[2] that is, a change in the opposite direction to what would be warranted by a more uniform structure of protection.

To complement the tariff liberalization scheme, import licensing was also gradually relaxed. From the original list of 1,304 import items banned or requiring 'prior approval' by the Central Bank and other government agencies, 263 were removed in 1981. Another 610 were taken off the list in early 1982, 87 in 1983 and the plan was to abolish the whole list by the end of 1984. The latter did not materialize, of course, as comprehensive controls on foreign exchange and imports were imposed as a full-scale foreign exchange crisis developed after August 1983.

Industrial Policy

It was recognized that the increased exposure to foreign competition would create adjustment problems for domestic producers who had long been operating under protected market conditions. Trade liberalization was therefore accompanied by 'revitalization' measures designed to help existing industries produce at lower cost through technical and credit assistance. An example, was the modernization and expansion plans for the textile industry involving 30 existing mills and one entirely new mill under a $450 million financing package. Other important industries were also identified and revitalization plans for some of them were prepared for financing and implementation. One problem faced by some of these industries, however, was been the depressed domestic market.

TABLE 3.1

Estimates of Effective Tariff Protection Rates in Philippine Manufacturing Industries, 1980 and 1985
(Per Cent)

Sector	*1980*	*1985*
Meat products	809.5	178.4
Dairy products	62.3	30.4
Rice milling	97.8	98.0
Sugar milling and refining	-1.1	-0.9
Processed fruits and vegetables	223.0	72.4
Processed fish and other seafoods	872.9	215.9
Other grain mill products	176.7	74.9
Bakery products	127.1	44.2
Cocoa, chocolate and sugar confectionery	71.2	30.1
Desiccated coconut products	-3.9	-2.6
Other manufactured foods	94.8	36.7
Liquors, wines, brewery and malt products	84.7	44.3
Soft drinks and carbonated water	127.5	69.5
Tobacco products	61.8	29.7
Textile and knitting mill products	61.4	36.0
Cordage, twine and other textile products	-9.3	-7.4
Footwear	-3.1	-2.2
Other wearing apparel	-10.5	-7.8
Other made-up textile goods	93.3	48.0
Lumber	-1.8	1.0
Plywood and veneer plants	-18.1	-13.4
Furniture and fixtures	-5.2	-4.0
Other wood, cane and cork products	-4.6	-3.4
Pulp, paper and paperboard manufacturing	47.5	29.3
Articles of pulp, paper and paperboard	158.5	58.1
Newspaper, periodicals, books and pamphlets	27.7	17.5
Printing, bookbinding and other allied products	51.5	28.6
Leather and leather products except for footwear and other wearing apparel	-10.7	-8.4
Rubber footwear	6.0	1.7
Tyres, tyre vulcanizing and recapping	54.0	39.5
Other rubber products	26.2	17.9
Basic industrial chemicals	14.0	12.8
Coconut oil	-0.7	-0.6
Other oils and fats	64.9	33.5
Fertilizer and lime	23.2	16.7
Paints, varnishes and related compounds	39.5	26.3
Plastic materials	44.3	23.2
Medicinal and pharmaceutical preparations	0.1	1.5

Sector	*1980*	*1985*
Soap and other washing and cleansing compounds	98.5	51.2
Other chemical products	47.0	34.3
Petroleum, refined and other petroleum products	12.4	12.6
Hydraulic cement	−10.1	−8.9
Structural clay and concrete products	69.4	56.7
Glass and glass products	54.6	41.7
Other non–metallic mineral products	54.3	36.7
Basic ferrous metal products	19.1	12.6
Cutlery, handtools and general hardware	52.0	55.7
Fabricated structural metal products	−10.3	−8.2
Heating apparatus, lighting and plumbing fixtures	83.6	63.6
Other fabricated metal products	68.4	50.2
Tractors and other agricultural machinery and equipment	27.0	13.7
Special industry machinery	16.3	21.0
General industry machinery and equipment (excluding electrical)	17.8	25.9
Office computing and accounting machines (excluding electrical)	12.7	15.4
Electrical industrial machinery and apparatus	38.5	35.2
Communication equipment excluding radio and television	47.9	10.9
Batteries	84.9	13.6
Electric lamps, fixtures, wires and wiring devices	25.5	16.0
Household radio, television receiving sets, phonos	35.5	12.0
Refrigeration and air–conditioning equipment	76.4	44.1
Other household electrical appliances and wares	77.9	34.1
Motor vehicles, engines, bodies and parts	31.9	26.8
Repair of motor vehicles (non–tradeable)	na	na
Shipbuilding and repairing	7.0	15.1
Other transport equipment	42.1	38.6
Miscellaneous manufactures	90.7	45.7
Average	70.3	31.0
Standard deviation	144.3	37.7
Coefficient of variation	2.05	1.22

Source: Bautista, 'The 1981-85 Tariff Changes and Effective Protection of Manufacturing Industries', *Journal of Philippine Development*, Vol. VIII, No. 1, 1981, pp. 11-12.

This made investment in new machinery and equipment seem unattractive and, as a result, demand tended to fall short of the amount of loanable funds made available for upgrading technology.

A very controversial aspect of industrial policy in the Philippines during this period concerns the so-called eleven major industrial projects which included the following: a copper smelter, a phosphate fertilizer plant, diesel engine manufacturing, cement industry rationalization, a coco-chemical complex, heavy engineering industries, an integrated steel project and an alcogas distillery. The government's justification in actively promoting these large-scale, capital-intensive, projects was that they 'would produce vital commodities and intermediate inputs at internationally competitive prices, induce the establishment of downstream labour-intensive industries, and enhance the country's technological capabilities'.[3] It was also announced that the projects would be financed mainly from private (domestic and foreign) funds and that they would be implemented only if they were economically viable. Unfortunately, insufficient information is publicly available to provide a basis for an independent evaluation of the economic feasibility of these projects.

The total cost of setting up the eleven projects has been estimated to be close to $4 billion (at 1981 prices). This would seem a large enough sum (about 10 per cent of the GNP in 1981) to be spent over a six-year period, to warrant a close examination of the macro-economic implications, especially for demand management and the inflation rate. Another source of anxiety was that, given the country's increasingly limited overall borrowing capacity, these large-scale capital-intensive projects might 'crowd out' imports of capital goods for light industry.

The only project which was completed by late 1983 was the copper smelter, which converts into copper cathodes the copper concentrates from all but one of the local copper mining companies (which have to contribute about 30 per cent of their current concentrate production). Foreign debt accounted for three-quarters of the funding and 32 per cent of the equity is held by a Japanese consortium (which is guaranteed a 9 per cent minimum annual dividend rate), 29 per cent from the local mining companies, and 5 per cent from the International Finance Corporation. A careful evaluation of this project has indicated that it is at best 'little better than marginal from an economic point of view'.[4]

The eleven projects would obviously not generate much employment and some of them, like the aluminium smelter and petrochemical complex, even import their principal raw materials. Very few, perhaps only those relying on domestic raw materials and not subject to rapid technological change, stand a chance of becoming commercially viable without heavy protection. With shelter from foreign competition, these projects will inevitably produce higher priced and lower quality intermediate and capital goods (compared to what can be imported) which will hinder rather than stimulate the development of downstream user industries. The latter are typically more labour-intensive and less energy-using and have a greater potential for exports.

It was also suggested that domestic raw materials for some of the eleven projects should be made available, as dictated by the government, at lower than world prices. This arrangement was applied to the copper smelter project, which effectively meant the taxation of local producers of copper concentrates. In any case, to give subsidies to certain projects on a selective basis was a deviation from the announced policy thrust towards trade liberalization. While it was true that the structure of protection at that time was biased against intermediate and capital goods production, conferring heavy subsidies to eleven such projects could benefit only a very small segment of the sector producing these goods. This was obviously an inferior substitute to dealing directly and adequately with the principal sources of the protection bias, namely tariff policy and the indirect tax system.

Fiscal and Financial Policies

Expansionary fiscal and monetary policies were adopted by the government in the early 1980s, aimed ostensibly at countering the recessionary pressures generated by the marked lowering of commodity export prices. As will be discussed below, this led to massive trade deficits accommodated by increased foreign borrowing. At the same time, some positive developments were taking place aimed at improving the structure of fiscal incentives and financial policies.

Increased neutrality in fiscal incentives for BOI-registered firms was an objective of the New Investment Incentives Policy Act, passed in early 1983, so that those incentives with known biases towards capital use (such as accelerated depreciation allowances and tariff exemption on imports of capital equipment) were withdrawn. Also a significant step toward promoting competition in the domestic market was the phasing out of the list of 'overcrowded industries', which included some 30 industries to which entry was restricted in the early 1970s.

Past financial policies had kept real interest rates low or even negative, especially during inflationary periods, thus encouraging capital intensity in both industry-mix and technology choice. Owing to the resulting excess demand for institutional credit, funds were rationed on criteria frequently unrelated to the economic feasibility of projects. In 1980-81, a comprehensive set of financial reforms was implemented aimed at promoting increased savings and better utilization of investment funds. Legal ceilings on nominal interest rates (effectively the prevailing rates) were gradually raised; and eventually, in July 1981, all interest rates were deregulated. This led to positive real interest rates, especially for longer-term time deposits. Also, restrictions in force earlier on the scope of the activities of financial institutions were reduced,[5] thus encouraging the consolidation of the banking system towards a few strong banks instead of a large number of family-owned, sectoral, banks.

Exchange Rate Policy

One important element of economic policy in the Philippines which has been the subject much controversy is the management of the price of foreign exchange. From the floating of the peso in February 1970 until the advent of the 1983 foreign exchange crisis, the authorities had maintained a flexible exchange rate policy, allowing the domestic currency to depreciate in nominal terms. The annual rate of depreciation varied from year to year; it exceeded 5 per cent but was less than 10 per cent in 1972, 1975 and 1982.

In the face of the sustained large deficits in the current account and the higher Philippine inflation rates relative to the country's trading partners during the period, it would seem surprising that the peso did not depreciate much more rapidly. The explanation lies in the capital account: the Philippines, having received relatively large amounts of foreign loans in the 1970s, faced no threat of depletion of international reserves and hence no immediate pressure to devalue.

Indeed, the extent of foreign borrowing since 1974 was such that Central Bank reserves even increased until 1980. However, when external financing slowed down and finally stopped (as happened in 1983), exchange rate adjustments could no longer be postponed. By late 1983, the official peso-United States dollar exchange rate stood at 14, the depreciation rate for the year (relative to the average exchange rate in 1982) being 30 per cent. That the scarcity value of foreign exchange is not reflected in the official exchange rate is suggested by the significantly higher black market exchange rate, which has ranged from 16-23 pesos to the dollar since October 1983. Based on time series estimates of the peso's real exchange rate, John H. Power found after the mid-1970s, 'virtually no evidence of an exchange rate policy response to the balance-of-payments crises'.[6]

In a sense, the external financing of the massive trade deficits since the mid-1970s distorted the real exchange rate,[7] artifically over-valuing the Philippine peso relative to other currencies. At the same time, the worsening terms of trade had a further depressing effect on the real exchange rate. These developments affected unfavourably the relative profitability of tradeable goods production and more than counter-balanced any positive influence on the real exchange rate of the trade liberalization measures implemented early in 1982.[8]

External Borrowing

The current account deficits in the 1970s were, of course, affected by the external shocks that had buffeted the Philippine economy since the oil crisis of 1973-74. The policy response to the adverse external developments and current account deficits was to borrow externally. In deciding to sustain the growth momentum initiated in the early 1970s, policymakers adopted a counter-cyclical strategy through expansionary fiscal and monetary policies. The annual rates of increases in government spending and money supply during 1974-80 averaged 22 and 18 per cent, respectively, which were much higher than their trend rates. While it probably made sense to seek foreign loans up to and including 1978 in view of the favourable borrowing terms (the London Interbank Offer Rate, LIBOR, was 9.3 per cent in 1978), adopting the same strategy in 1981 (when LIBOR had increased to 16 per cent) proved to be very costly in terms of the country's debt burden.

What is worse, the investments made were not paying off. Government financial institutions had financed many projects of doubtful economic viability whose proponents were frequently persons with strong political connections. Hotel building and other tourist related projects, implemented in the mid-1970s, are a prominent example. Hotels were under-utilized from their completion and ownership and management of most of the 14 five-star hotels constructed in 1975-76 have since been taken over by the Development Bank of the Philippines, a government institution.[9] By 1982 foreign borrowing had reached a record 8.5 per cent of GNP and the government deficit was at an unprecedented 4.3 per cent of GNP. It is also not a coincidence that the public sector's share in total external debt rose from 40 per cent in 1971 to 56 per cent in 1982.

In absolute terms foreign borrowing by the private sector also increased significantly — by 20 per cent annually during

1973-82 on average (or, deflated by the import price index, by 8 per cent). This can be attributed in part to the undervaluation of the exchange rate which made foreign capital more attractive than domestic sources. Since the government generally guaranteed debt repayment, foreign lending to the private sector was given additional encouragement. As Helen Hughes has pointed out, easy access to external capital under conditions of restricted trade often leads to excessive foreign borrowing.[10]

From 1981 it was no longer possible to finance current account deficits from foreign loans and this meant that there was a significant drawing down of Central Bank reserves. Moreover, in view of the tightness of the international financial market, there was increasing difficulty in obtaining long-term loans. In 1982, the amount of short-term capital inflows was about three times what it had been in 1979 (reaching $12.1 billion) and the ratio of short-term debt to total outstanding debt rose sharply from 18.6 per cent to 25.6 per cent. Normally, short-term loans were being 'rolled over' on a three to twelve-month basis. However, as foreign bank lenders became more apprehensive about the country's mounting indebtedness, repayment of short-term loans was increasingly being requested. The present debt crisis has arisen essentially because lenders have stopped rolling over short-term loans because of the political instability since August 1983. To compound the problem, there was also a massive capital flight, estimated at $200 million, following the Benigno Aquino assassination. The $2.7 billion current account deficit incurred in 1983 (representing a record 8 per cent of GNP) had to be financed from international reserves, which slumped to a level equivalent to less than one month's imports by mid-October. This represented, by any standards, a foreign exchange crisis.

Foreign exchange and import controls were imposed in October 1983, signalling an emergency retreat from the trade liberalization programme. The Central Bank required all commercial banks to hand in their foreign exchange receipts so that priority imports and other payments could be made.

The priority listing of foreign exchange payments during the crisis included the following: oil imports, maturing official development assistance loans, trade-related payments for inputs to export industries, raw materials for vital domestic industries, including foodgrains, interest on foreign bank loans and inter-bank loans and trade-related credits.

These controls on foreign exchange and imports superseded, therefore, the scheduled lifting of import bans in 1984 under the trade liberalization programme. Tariff rate revisions were not, however, substantially affected. As a revenue measure and also to curtail imports, a 5 per cent general import tax was imposed in November 1983 but this did not have a long-term distortionary effect in view of its temporary and across-the-board character. It was also announced that the eleven major industrial projects were 'on hold' and some of them were later abandoned. It remains to be seen how these and other components of the industrial structural adjustment programme will be dealt with by President Aquino's Government.

Concluding Remarks

It is unfortunate that the 1981 attempt at trade liberalization in the Philippines took place during a period of extremely adverse conditions in the external economic environment. The deterioration in the country's terms of trade was especially severe: with 1972 as base year the terms of trade index declined to 71 in 1977 and to an average of 60 during 1981-83. The depth and length of the world recession in the early 1980s would also have imposed an effective constraint on the country's ability to expand exports and reduce trade deficits.

Unfavourable external circumstances have undoubtedly been an important influence in the Philippines' economic performance since the early 1970s. They have also hampered the implementation of trade liberalization policies and contributed to the severe balance-of-payments problem. This, however, does not tell the whole story. The role of domestic policies was also significant. The decision to adopt expansionary macro-economic policies, which frequently bordered on profligate demand management, led to rapid increases in imports. This was not matched by a commensurate expansion of exports and heavy external borrowing was therefore necessary. The poor export performance was partly because of depressed foreign demand and partly because of the relative uncompetitiveness of domestic industry. The latter, in turn, was due to 'market price distortions (arising) from ... trade and industrial policies (which) not only hampered the growth of non-traditional exports, but also undermind the efficiency of translating a high level of investment into growth'.[11]

Finally, it may be noted that the 1983 foreign exchange crisis bears a close similarity to the 1969 experience. As Professor Baldwin has concluded in his anaysis of the 1966-69 period, it 'demonstrates that Philippine economic development cannot long be sustained at a high rate unless there is also a high growth rate of export earnings. Extensive credit creation and foreign borrowing can initiate periods of prosperity; but unless these measures are accompanied by exchange-rate (and other) policies designed to maintain a vigorous export sector, these periods of expanding economic activity are doomed to end suddenly as balance-of-payments problems build up to a crisis'.[12] The same statement could be made in reference to the 1981-83 period.

NOTES AND REFERENCES

1. These estimates as well as those contained in Table 3.1, are based on tariffs as the only determinant of effective protection; they abstract from the effects of other relevant policy instruments such as indirect taxes and fiscal incentives which at the time the EPR calculations were made, were still being reviewed and had not assumed any definite shape for 1985.

2. From 29 per cent in 1980 to 14 per cent in 1985 for intermediate goods, and from 24 to 20 per cent for capital goods.

3. *Five-Year Philippine Development Plan, 1978-1982* (updated for 1981 and 1982) (Manila: National Economic Development Authority) p. 13.

4. Craig Emerson and Peter G. Warr, 'Economic Evaluation of

Mineral Processing Projects: a Case Study of Copper Smelting in the Philippines', *Philippine Economic Journal*, Manila, Vol. XX, No. 2, 1981, pp. 175-97.

5. In particular, qualified commercial banks have been allowed to engage in equity investment, savings banks have been given full domestic banking powers and rural banks permitted to engage in branch banking.

6. Power, *Response of Payments Crises in the 1970s: Korea and the Philippines*, Staff Paper Series No. 83-05 (Manila: Philippine Institute for Development Studies, 1983) p. 26.

7. The real exchange rate is defined as the relative prices of traded goods (that is, exports and import substitutes) to non-traded goods.

8. For details see Bautista, *Production Incentives in Philippine Agriculture: Effects of Trade and Exchange Rate Policies*, Research Report No. 59 (Washington: International Food Policy Research Institute, 1987).

9. The conversion of government loans to equity became a common form of rescuing financially troubled firms. Thus, in mid-1983, the Development Bank of the Philippines owned or managed 73 large once-private firms; other public corporations, such as the National Development Company and the Philippine National Bank, also took over many firms threatened by failure in which the government had a substantial financial interest.

10. Helen Hughes, 'External Debt Problems of Developing Countries' in Bautista and Saja Naya (eds), *Energy and Structural Change in the Asia-Pacific Region* (Manila: Philippine Institute for Development Studies and Asian Development Bank, 1984).

11. Power, *op. cit.*, p. 27.

12. Baldwin, *op. cit.*, p. 74.

Chapter 4

Political Aspects of Trade Liberalization

UNTIL the late 1950s there was little recognition, even among serious students of Philippine economic development, of the distortionary effects of post-war trade and exchange rate policies. From the viewpoint of policy makers there was also no apparent cause for concern. The manufacturing sector was growing rapidly as investments in industries producing import substitutes responded well to the increased profitability provided by the trade controls and peso over-valuation. Balance-of-payments difficulties, as well as charges of corruption and poor administration of the control system together with pressures from exporters for a favourable exchange rate, forced the lifting of controls and the currency devaluation in the early 1960s. It was, however, made clear 'to the business community that the government ... wished merely to substitute tariff protection for the protection provided by the control system'.[1] That the then President Diosdado Macapagal had to include such a statement in his state-of-the-nation address in 1962 is an indication of the strong political presence of the new industrialists at that time. Indeed, this class of entrepreneurs was well represented in the Cabinet of the government of that period.

Transition to Export Promotion Policies

The lifting of controls did not significantly affect the existing structure of protection. What it did do was to effect a transfer of income from importers to the government, the scarcity premium for imports (or rent accruing to the importers) having been transformed into tariff revenue. This led to a reduction in the opportunities for corruption in government and for rent-seeking activities in the private sector, both socially unproductive and wasteful of scarce resources (especially entrepreneurship).

Exporters benefited, of course, from the 1962 peso devaluation, since the same foreign exchange receipts would have a proportionately higher peso value. The increased export profitability was eroded over time, however, by the high inflation rate throughout most of the 1960s, a departure from the remarkable stability of the general price level in the 1950s. Moreover, continued industrial import restrictions, through high tariffs, served to defend the exchange rate at an increasingly unrealistic level.

Soon after assuming power in 1966, the Marcos Administration embarked on an expansionary programme to spur industrial growth. Compared to previous administrations in the post-war period, greater attention was given to promoting exports. At that time, the favourable experiences of some of the North-east Asian countries such as Hong Kong, South Korea, Taiwan, and Singapore, where the industrial development programmes were geared towards export markets, began to be appreciated in the Philippines. Government policy was also being influenced by contemporary academic discussions about the penalties being imposed on export-oriented industries by the existing import-substitution policies. The appointment in 1970 of a young university professor (and leading critic of inward-oriented industrialization)[2] as head of the government's planning office indicated increased favour within the Marcos Government towards the role of foreign trade in Philippine economic development.

Interest Groups

Indeed, in the late 1960s and in the following decade, the number of senior government officials with strong academic backgrounds (and post-graduate degrees in leading universities in the United States) increased significantly. These 'technocrats', possessing an international perspective on economic development issues, were sympathetic to the idea of export-led industrial growth and they became the *de facto* political representatives of export producers, especially of non-traditional labour-intensive manufactured products in which the country was thought to have comparative advantage. Export producers comprised a very small class of industrial entrepreneurs at that time relative, that is, to other producer groups being favoured by the protectionist foreign trade regime.

Labour as an interest group took a somewhat indifferent attitude toward the public debate on industrial development strategy. As Gonzaro Jurado *et al.* have pointed out, 'ever since the policy of export-led industrialization was enunciated, organized labour has never made a clear-cut statement of affirmation or criticism of this strategy'.[3] Unorganized labour, which accounts for the majority of the labour force has, of course, little voice. Yet it is this very group that presumably would benefit most from a development strategy that serves to promote the utilization of the country's abundant resources. Government economic planners have tended to regard the earnings of organized labour, particularly earnings of unskilled labour, as being artificially high, owing to statutory minimum wage legislation and social security benefits which, together with the biases of existing trade and industrial policies, are alleged to have inhibited the growth of industrial employment.

The objectives of increased employment and higher incomes promised by export-led industrialization are consistent with the declared goals of organized labour. The need for various restrictions on workers' rights to self-organization and the right to strike which the government had imposed (under martial law) in 1972 was, however, open to question. Some of the restrictions applied with particular force to labour-intensive export-oriented industries, considered 'strategic' by the government. The apparent preference on the part of organized labour for capital-intensive industries could perhaps be rationalized on the basis of the vulnerability of such industries to strikes and other labour disruptions.

Labour leaders found support in the writings of a small but articulate group of self-styled economic nationalists, some of them with vested interests in having the industrial import-substitution drive sustained. They advocated an approach to industrialization in the style advocated by the influential Indian theorist of central planning, P.C. Mahalanobis, that is, emphasis on the establishment of heavy industries in order to make the country 'self-reliant' and the manufacturing sector free from 'foreign domination'. It never occurred to them that protection of one set of industries could be disadvantageous to others.

The implementation of land reform from 1972 weakened the political role of rice and corn farmers within the land-owning class. Producers of the traditional export crops (principally coconut and sugar) were a more potent influence on government policy, having successfully resisted land reform and waged a strong campaign for a more realistic exchange rate policy during the 1950s. Some of them had invested heavily in industries producing import substitutes and resented the growing emphasis in the government on the promotion of non-traditional industrial exports.

The hesitant and limited steps taken during the 1970s to correct the highly protective and distorted trade and industrial policies can be interpreted as reflecting the political compromises among contending interest groups and a rather weak conviction at the highest policy level of the urgency of trade liberalization. Policy advice from both local and foreign sources was not lacking. At the request of the Philippine Government, the International Labour Office (ILO) sponsored a 'comprehensive employment strategy mission' to Manila in 1973, headed by Professor Gustav Ranis of Yale University. The mission's report,[4] which was well-publicized locally and much discussed in government and academic circles, emphasized the critical importance for the future sustained growth of the Philippine economy of 'the diversification of exports towards new labour-intensive industrial goods' and 'of trade liberalization and related policies'.[5] In 1976 the World Bank also published, as part of its country study series, a report on Philippine development problems and prospects,[6] which virtually repeated the recommendations of the ILO mission concerning trade and industrial policies. Both reports were critical of the adoption of counter-incentives to offset in a selective manner the biases of the protective system. The phasing out of fiscal incentives given to BOI-registered enterprises, including those under the Export Incentives Act of 1970, was specifically recommended by the ILO mission. The question being raised implicitly was whether government bureaucrats were capable of predicting the successful export industries of the future. It was also made clear that the system of BOI incentives was not reaching the small and regionally dispersed enterprises, especially in the rural areas, whose participation in the growth process was deemed critical to the export-bid development strategy.

The proposal to remove BOI incentives was naturally not received favourably by the engineers and business trained managers who dominated the bureaucracy at the Board of Investments. It is a reflection of their strong influence on policy making that this recommendation was not even seriously considered. Whatever penalties to export production then existed, they were seen by the BOI as manageable on a case-to-case basis (contrary to what economic analysis had concluded) and the Board continued to promote investments in areas indicated in its annual *Export Priorities Plan*.

The 1981-85 Trade Liberalization Episode

A more serious commitment by the government to trade liberalization appears to have been made in the early 1980s. The scheduled tariff revisions during 1981-85 and the relaxation of import licensing from 1981-83 were substantial;

it was surprising to outsiders how quickly the trade liberalization measures were formulated and adopted by the government, given the political realities at the time.

The first point to note is that the technocrats who were sympathetic to a liberalized trade regime were still influential in policy making during 1979-80, when the comprehensive review of the existing protective system was undertaken by the government. The country's macro-economic performance during the 1970s — a period of increased instability in the external economic environment — was better than might have been expected and marked expansion and diversification of exports was seen to have made a significant contribution.

Second, the World Bank had just introduced a new lending arrangement in which the extension of so-called structural adjustment loans to developing countries was made conditional on the implementation of policy reforms to improve the efficiency of resource use and promote the international competitiveness of domestic industries. As the Philippine Government had to cope at the time with the oil price shock of 1979-80 and other unfavourable external developments, it was only too willing to receive the $200 million loan (granted in September 1980) and, as a condition, to implement an industrial structural adjustment programme. It was regarded as only the first of a series of structural adjustment loans. (A $300 million loan, focussing on the energy sector and industrial incentives, was signed in April 1983. A third structural adjustment loan, estimated at $300-350 million involves reforms in agricultural credit, incentives and institutions.) This would seem to indicate that the provision of substantial financial and technical assistance at a time of need can be made to exercise considerable leverage in generating the political will to adopt trade liberalization measures; as already indicated, earlier suggestions from the ILO and the World Bank had failed to evoke such a favourable response.

It was certainly not all smooth sailing for the proponents of trade liberalization within the government. Sectoral interests of individual ministries and other government offices had to be given due consideration; some officials tended to adopt very rigid positions concerning the relaxation of import licensing or tariff reductions on imports competitive with domestic products perceived to be of strategic importance. Industrial associations, which had previously taken an indifferent attitude to the deliberations at public hearings conducted by the Tariff Commission because 'nothing of consequence ever gets done', soon realized that this time the government plans for tariff reform were serious and that they had to wage an active campaign (and where possible, pull political strings) to protect their interests. Some multinational firms which were established in the 1950s to secure the domestic market and which continued to benefit from the protective trade regime, threatened to reduce production levels or to discontinue local operations altogether, always emphasizing that many workers would be laid off. Additional difficulties were presented by the fact that major companies in some of the most protected industries had, on their Boards of Directors, some senior officials of government ministries and of financial institutions with considerable influence on government decisions.

Inevitably, there was an abundance of conflicting interests, the resolution of which took many forms at different levels. At inter-agency technical meetings concessions were made by lowering tariff rates on intermediate and capital goods used by some industries whose nominal protection was being reduced. This explains why effective protection rates for intermediate and capital goods declined even after the completion of the tariff reform programme in 1985. Some government officials with a vested interest in keeping heavy protection for certain industries managed to win their case in higher level meetings.

A striking example of the political weight of some industrial associations was the reported reimposition of government restrictions on imports of a number of durable consumer goods, mostly household appliances, two weeks after a Central Bank circular had been issued removing the 24 items involved from the list of banned imports. According to the news report, 'the sudden policy shift was in reaction to strong criticism from local household appliance manufacturers'.[7] Not as well publicized but an equally good illustration of the politics behind the trade liberalization measures, was the issuing of a Presidential executive order (one of several that enacted the schedule of tariff changes over the period 1981-85) which, in accommodating requests from representatives of the food processing industry, revised some of the tariff rates contained in another executive order issued only a few months earlier.

The end result, understandably, was not a policy reform programme promising a complete liberalization of the country's foreign trade regime. As indicated in Chapter 3, there is still plenty of scope for further improvement of the tariff system even though the 1985 programme has been completed. It would have also been interesting to see how the liberalization of import licensing might have proceeded had the debt-service crisis not appeared in 1983.

In comparison with earlier attempts to liberalize the foreign trade regime, however, the attempt made in 1981-85 can be considered quite significant. It was made possible only because there appeared to be a strong commitment to trade liberalization at the highest policy level (and indeed quotations from Presidential memoranda and policy speeches served as ammunition for the proponents in discussions within the government). This commitment in turn was the result of two important influences.

> First, the increasing perception of the gains to be obtained from export expansion and of the effective penalties imposed on export producers by the protective and distorted trade policy (and here the technocrats played an important role in shaping that perception).
>
> Second, and perhaps equally important, the World Bank offer of financial and technical assistance in the form of a series of structural adjustment loans at a time of adverse external developments and declining opportunities for the foreign borrowing that was needed to sustain the government's high growth strategy.

As indicated earlier, trade liberalization was one component of a wider programme to restructure domestic industry. Indeed, the structural adjustment loan funds were designed to finance the upgrading of old plants and the revitalization of existing industries that had grown up in a climate of excessive protection. Another component of the industrial restructuring programme was the promotion of the eleven major industrial products which, as argued above, would seem to be incompatible with the larger policy thrust toward achieving gains in allocative efficiency and international competitiveness. This programme also threatened the integrity of the trade liberalization programme since few, if any, of the eleven projects could expect to survive without protection from foreign competition. The considerable criticism of many of the projects in public discussions and in discussions among government officials and with World Bank missions had, however, not moved the sole proponent — the Ministry of Trade and Industry — to withdraw any of the projects. In the end, even the World Bank delegation simply avoided any confrontation on this issue. It is an indication of the Ministry's powerful influence in policy making that none of the eleven major industrial projects was shelved prior to the emergence of the foreign exchange crisis in 1983. In like manner, its policy influence in the post-crisis period will be a major determinant of the extent to which the projects are revived and their implementation actively promoted by the new government. In view of the increasing leverage of the IMF and the World Bank, however, it is perhaps safe to assume that potential 'white elephants' of this sort will not be allowed to crowd out other development projects which have less severe financing requirements.

Political Elements in the Economic Crisis

As already indicated, both political and economic factors contributed significantly to the emergence of the foreign exchange crisis in late 1983. The term 'economic crisis' has since been increasingly used and with good reason. The Philippine economy contracted by nearly 10 per cent in the following two years; indeed, GNP per capita in 1985 declined to the 1975 level. A 'political crisis' for the Marcos regime soon developed, leading to the February 1986 change in government, with Corazon Aquino as the new President. Clearly, in addition to rebuilding democracy, the major challenge faced by the new government is to find the route to rapid economic recovery and long-run stable growth.

The personal popularity of President Aquino and new-found credibility of the government, sorely missing in the last few years of the Marcos regime, augur well for meeting this challenge. At the same time, some political problems that confront the new government could be distracting and may slow down policy efforts toward economic reform; also, perceptions of political instability can rapidly erode business confidence. The first problem concerns the need to deal with the insurgency movement that President Aquino believes can be won over through peaceful negotiations. Is the strategy of removing the economic injustices that sustained the movement in the past more effective in putting an end to the insurgency than the military solution being advocated by some of her advisers? In any case, it does not seem likely that the problem can be solved overnight.

The second problem will arise in dealing with the right and left wing political groups. The new government has not only to overcome the political challenges from the right which resisted administrative and economic reforms in the past but also from left-wing politicians who would like to assert more governmental control over the economy, to protect inefficient industries from foreign competition and to keep out the IMF, the World Bank and foreign investors. The ideological and political differences within President Aquino's own government present a third problem which will need to be resolved before concerted efforts can be exerted on any strategy to promote economic recovery and long-run growth. Finally, there is a need to improve government decision making and administration beyond the Cabinet down to the regional and local government levels so that policy changes can be effectively implemented.

NOTES AND REFERENCES

1. Baldwin, *op. cit.*, p. 62.

2. When he was named Chairman of the National Economic Council (NEC), Gerardo P. Sicat was in his mid-30s writing a monograph on Philippine industrialization and trade policies in collaboration with a visiting American professor, John H. Power. (Their work, cited in Chapter 2, was published in 1971 as one of the country studies in the research project sponsored by the Organisation for Economic Cooperation and Development and coordinated by Ian Little, Tibor Scitovsky, and Maurice Scott.) In 1974 other government offices with development planning functions were merged with NEC to form the National Economic and Development Authority. Dr Sicat was appointed its first Director-General with Cabinet rank as Minister of Economic Planning. He held this post until July 1981.

3. Jurado *et al.*, *op. cit.*, p. 83.

4. *Sharing in Development in the Philippines* (Geneva: International Labour Office, 1974).

5. *Ibid.*, pp. xxv and 109.

6. *The Philippines: Development Problems and Prospects* (Washington: Johns Hopkins Press, for the World Bank, 1976).

7. *Times Journal*, Manila, 4 March 1982.

Chapter 5

The International Economic Environment

IT IS often argued that the export-led development strategy, which worked for the newly-industrializing countries (NICs) in the 1960s, is inappropriate for other developing countries in the international economic environment of the 1980s. To quote from a recent study on Philippine trade policy:

> 'The international environment which nurtured the NICs had radically changed by the 1970s. A major recession had taken over the major trading countries, severely curtailing their demand for imports. Protective barriers had been set up in the industrialized countries, shutting out much of the products of the aspiring NICs from export markets... There is clearly a need for a modification of industrialization strategy to take into account the current features of the international economy.'[1]

While a pro-trade perspective is implicit in any trade liberalization effort, the basic objective, it must be emphasized, is to help rationalize a country's production structure and provide for effective competition so that scarce resources can be allocated and utilized more efficiently. This is a desirable objective regardless of external developments. The possibility of a protracted decline in foreign demand does not imply that the efficiency with which domestic resources are being used no longer matters. The need to import a large part of the production goods used by domestic industries gives added urgency to the need to earn and save foreign exchange efficiently; this would hardly be helped by a return to protectionist policies. The solution to the problem of the increase in trade restrictions in some industrialized countries, is not to turn inward and heavily protect the domestic market which past Philippine experience has shown to be very costly. The better means is to seek and expand export markets elsewhere.

It goes without saying, however, that recovery in the economies of present and potential trading partners together with the liberalization of trade in those economies would help to produce a more favourable trade performance for the Philippines. It would also greatly contribute to the solution of the Philippines' debt-servicing and balance-of-payments problems as well as helping to overcome domestic resistance to policy reform towards trade liberalization.

Recession and Protectionism in the Markets of Developed Countries

It is necessary to distinguish between the effects of recession and those of protection in the developed countries (which constitute at present the principal markets for most of the exports of developing countries). A recession is a cyclical and not a long-term phenomenon and its demand-reducing effects will normally be reversed in the subsequent recovery. On the other hand, recessionary conditions may induce the setting up of protective barriers and it is not necessarily the case that those barriers will automatically be removed in the recovery — that is to say, they can become a permanent part of a country's trade policy. The effects of a recession on the demand for imports, however, are presumably across-the-board whereas protection in the markets of developed countries has in practice been directed at specific targets in terms of imported products and supplying countries.[2] The means by which these two causes of demand contraction for developing-country exports can be addressed would also differ.

In the Philippine context, the two dominant trade partners, Japan and the United States,[3] appear to have recovered from the recessionary conditions of the early 1980s. Protectionist sentiments have not eased significantly, however, at least as far as products of export interest to the Philippines are concerned. In 1983 almost a quarter of the country's total export revenue of $5 billion came from 40 products that faced some form of protectionist measure in 18 countries.[4] Thirty-seven export products, earning $578 million, were subject to various artificial barriers in Japan; United States non-tariff measures affected 21 export commodities which earned $125 million; while European Community protectionist policies affected 26 Philippine products which earned $377 million in 1983.

Non-traditional labour-intensive exports are being promoted by the Philippine government to diversify exports and generate productive employment. It is, however, precisely this class of exports from less-developed countries that has been the major target of protectionist measures in developed-country markets. Apart from garments and textiles, for which bilateral trade agreements have been negotiated under the Multi-fibre Arrangement (MFA) since 1974, Philippine exports of footwear, electronic products, processed food items, wood products, and handicrafts have been subject to a plethora of import restrictions in member countries of the OECD.

The severest protectionism against developing countries has been imposed under the MFA, especially since the first renewal of the MFA in 1977, which tightened up on imports from low-cost countries. The third MFA, which was agreed in December 1981, represents 'another turn of the protectionist screw' as does the fourth, agreed in July 1986.[5] Of particular concern to the Philippines, which contributes a scant 2 per cent of total developing country exports of garments and textiles, is the new feature of an 'anti-surge mechanism' to limit full utilization of previously unutilized quotas and further restrictions in the use of flexibility conditions.

Particular difficulty has been experienced by Philippine exporters of non-traditional labour-intensive manufactured products in penetrating the Japanese market. This may seem surprising given that (a) Japan's comparative advantage in labour-intensive manufactures has been considerably weakened by increasing labour scarcity and rapid rises in wages and (b) there has been a remarkable growth of Philippine exports of such products in other developed-country markets, including the United States. While the Japanese Government, since January 1982, has reduced tariff rates on an increasing number of import commodities (ahead of the original plan set during the Tokyo Round of multilateral trade negotiations) and also lowered some non-tariff barriers, this was apparently intended to soothe growing tension over trade with the United States and the European Community.

Asian developing countries share the Western view 'that Japan isn't as open to foreign products as other industrial nations. But because their objections don't seem to carry quite the same weight with Tokyo, they're glad to let Japan's Western allies do the shouting. Asian exporters hope that, under multilateral trade rules, anything Japan does for the West will help them out too.'[6] This would seem an unnecessarily passive stance which may not benefit the Philippines very much. The specific products which the Philippine exporters are concerned about (garments, wood manufactures and leather products) differ from those which are of concern to the exporters of the United States and the European Community. A general relaxation of existing 'indirect, covert, administrative controls' in Japan would be necessary for Philippine and other producers of labour-intensive export products in the Association of South East Asian Nations (ASEAN) to make significant inroads in the Japanese market.

The share of Philippine manufactured exports going to other important developed-country markets is insignificant. Australia, Canada, and New Zealand, three Pacific Basin countries, are widely considered to be very restrictive with respect to imports of labour-intensive manufactures.

The tariff structure in developed countries is only one of the factors which makes it difficult for the Philippines to pursue successfully the expansion of exports of processed primary products. There are other problems in that the high capital, scale and energy intensity of existing technology for most resource-based industries could offset completely the Philippines' advantage in producing the primary product. Market prospects are also uncertain in view of investments which have already been made in the processing industries by developed countries using imported primary products. In addition, developed countries tend to use discriminatory tariffs against imports of processed commodities. According to the study by Alexander J. Yeats involving 21 agricultural and mineral products, developed-country tariffs add only 3 per cent to the cost of imported materials but they increase to more than 20 per cent along the 'processing chain'.[7] These higher rates serve to encourage domestic firms in the industrialized countries to import raw materials for processing in the home market.

Trade with the NICs and Other ASEAN Countries

In terms of future sources of export growth, the involvement of the Asian NICs in trade liberalization would also be potentially beneficial to the Philippines and other Asian 'near-NICs'.[8] The success of the 'near-NICs' in expanding labour-intensive manufactured exports in the medium term is contingent, among other things, on the continued evolution of the NICs' comparative advantage into more sophisticated industrial products. In the process, the contribution of the NICs to the world market for labour-intensive manufactures will be reduced and, within their domestic markets, import demand for such products will increase.

Two-fifths of the total imports from the Philippines of Singapore and Hong Kong (which have the most liberal foreign trade regimes among Pacific Basin countries) are already in labour-intensive manufactures. Why the Philippines has not sold proportionately as much of these products to Taiwan and South Korea (only about 8 per cent each) is presumably related to the trade restrictions in these two countries. A lowering of import barriers, especially non-tariff barriers, by the NICs would not only reduce a source of friction but would also 'contribute to a more stable world trading system by signifying the readiness of the more advanced developing countries progressively to adhere to the rules and obligations applying to the more mature trading nations.'[9]

The degree to which the NICs are willing to open up their domestic markets will have implications not only for the development prospects of the Philippines and other near-NICs but also for the future growth of the NICs themselves. Thus, increased access to such markets by the ASEAN countries, together with their own structural adjustment efforts (which should lead to expanded NIC exports to the ASEAN countries),[10] could provide the stimulus necessary to sustain rapid industrial growth in these two developing-country groups which between them have the world's fastest growing national incomes.[11]

General trade liberalization among the Asian NICs could also be expected to open up possibilities for increased agricultural and mining exports from the resource-rich ASEAN countries. The relatively resource-poor Asian NICs have high levels of protection for primary products, especially agricultural food commodities.[12] Some industries which are both resource and technology intensive, however, present difficulties for complementary production and trade, especially if they require the construction of integrated plants (or 'complexes'); also, because these are often basic industries, individual countries may wish to develop them themselves, seeking to be self-reliant in the production of so-called critical products. In the Philippine context, this is well illustrated by some of the eleven major industrial projects described in Chapter 3. Harmonization of investment plans and trade policies among the ASEAN countries and the Asian NICs is essential if this type of problem is to be overcome.

Within the ASEAN, a preferential trading arrangement (PTA) has been in existence for some time but the impact of this regional trade liberalization programme has yet to be felt by the member countries. This is because of unwillingness to expose their domestic markets to regional competition, as reflected in the fact that intra-ASEAN trade concessions have been kept strictly to marginal imports. Also, because of the relative success that they have enjoyed until the 1980s in expanding exports to countries outside the region, ASEAN countries have not been overly aggressive in promoting intra-regional trade. But, if their access to foreign markets becomes increasingly limited, it can be expected that pressures for intra-ASEAN trade liberalization will increase.

Although there could be ill effects from possible trade diversion, the expansion of Philippine trade through preferential arrangements with other ASEAN countries, with the Asian NICs and with other developing countries, would confer dynamic, learning and competitive benefits. The development of trade among less developed countries themselves cannot, of course, fully compensate for the slower growth of demand in, and uncertainty of access to, the markets in developed counties. Clearly, a more generalized liberal trading system would be preferable, ideally in the broader international context, or, if the European Community is unwilling to participate in the global lowering of trade barriers (given the prevailing mood in that part of the world), at least among the developing and developed countries in the Pacific Basin.

The Debt Servicing Problem

The need for improved access to foreign markets is accentuated in the Philippine case by its debt servicing problem, whatever terms are eventually negotiated on the repayment of the country's $26 billion outstanding debt. In turn, the debt service burden depends first, on the extent to which foreign bank lenders are willing to offer concessions to the Philippines to make repayment terms easier and, second, on the behaviour of interest rates in world financial markets. The lighter the debt service burden is, the more tolerable will be the economic and political strains associated with trade liberalization, thus increasing the likelihood of success.

Another potentially important external influence is the movement of the country's terms of trade. The Philippines appears particularly vulnerable to sharp increases in the world price of oil (in view of its heavy dependence on imported oil) and to recessionary conditions in the industrialized countries (which depress world prices of Philippine commodity exports). This was reflected in the drastic deterioration of the terms of trade during 1974-77 and 1979-82 already noted. Ideally, short-run swings in the trade balance caused by fluctuations in the terms of trade should be met from foreign exchange reserves or short-term borrowing, thus avoiding the need to directly curtail imports or to adjust the exchange rate. Again, international lending can contribute to the trade liberalization effort of a country whose foreign exchange reserves are inadequate to cope with year-to-year changes in its terms of trade.

Generally, individual debtor LDCs have no control over such outside factors as interest rate movements and changes in the world prices of their principal imports and exports which affect their ability to service external debt. This would seem to argue for writing into the agreements with foreign creditors flexibility provisions that will assure the debtor countries some protection from adverse external developments.[13] Otherwise, further import restrictions will be needed to meet repayment obligations adding to the economic and political difficulties of the debtor LDCs. It has been estimated, for example, that a one per cent increase in United States interest rates and a one dollar per barrel increase in the import price of oil would lead, respectively, to a $90 million annual rise in Philippine debt-service obligations and to an additional $52 million increase in its trade deficit.[14]

In any balance-of-payments adjustment, export expansion through trade liberalization, which is growth-inducing, is more efficient than cutting imports through austerity measures, which is growth-inhibiting. This is well demonstrated in the post-World War II experience of the Philippines which was discussed earlier. It is clearly in the long-run interest of both debtor countries and foreign bank creditors that the scope for pursuing the former strategy is not reduced by unanticipated problems in the external economic environment.

Role of International Organizations

Both protectionist measures in importing developed countries and counter measures in exporting developing countries have generally been in conflict with the GATT principles and, along with growing bilateralism and regionalism in recent trading arrangements, they represent a threat to the multilateral trading system.

The United States, the European Community and Japan are widely known to 'dominate the GATT so much that other members feel they have little meaningful voice.'[15] The special treatment of textiles and garments, as well as government interventions (and widespread flouting of the GATT safeguard rules) in trade in agriculture, consumer electronics, footwear, shipbuilding, steel, *et cetera*, have increasingly weakened the effectiveness and relevance of the GATT in the eyes of developing countries. For example, the Philippines and other ASEAN countries have openly criticized the European Community for its unwillingness to bring its common agricultural policy within the provisions of the GATT (in particular, the protection of sugar) and the United States for the discriminatory character of its Caribbean Basin Initiative. Recent efforts to liberalize import restrictions by the Japanese government in an effort to appease its American and European trade partners without including the neighbouring ASEAN countries in the benefits of the liberalization, also convey the impression that the GATT is of little relevance. The industrialized countries seem to be able to negotiate settlement of trade conflicts on their own and to make deals among themselves outside the GATT system.

Of course, governments of developing countries have certainly not been immune to bilateral and regional arrangements which restrict trade with third countries in contravention of the GATT provisions. Systems of protection have also been established which are specifically tailored to individual sectors. Part of the reason lies in the political need to take action to safeguard such sectors from the protectionist measures adopted in developed countries. Nevertheless, until the major signatories themselves demonstrate a willingness to adhere to the GATT rules and principles, it would be hypocritical for them to insist on full compliance by the developing countries. This does not imply, however, that it is not in the interest of small developing countries like the Philippines to work towards the improvement of the international trading system, particularly in support of proposals for general applicability of the GATT rules and principles.

The Philippines actively participates in the meetings and deliberations of the GATT committees, such as those on Trade and Development, Trade in Agricultural Products, Quantitative Restrictions and Other Non-Tariff Measures, Balance-of-Payments Restrictions, Import Licensing and Technical Barriers to Trade, and it has observer status in the other code committees. It is a signatory to the GATT Codes on Import Licensing Regulations and on Technical Barriers to Trade and plans to accede to the Code on Subsidies. The latter move 'is primarily intended to counter current lobbying in the United States for the imposition of countervailing duties on imports of garment products from 13 developing countries, including the Philippines'.[16]

The foreign exchange crisis in the Philippines increased the political leverage of the World Bank and the IMF and commitments made by the government to these two international organizations are more likely to be complied with than its commitments as a GATT member. An illustration is provided by the long-standing practice of levying on imported consumer durables higher excise tax rates relative to similar local products. The government resisted for some time suggestions from the GATT to remove this source of trade restriction but it gave in to World Bank pressure to do so as part of the policy reforms accompanying the industrial restructuring programme.

As already explained, in offering to provide financial and technical assistance through its structural adjustment loans, the World Bank was instrumental in persuading the Philippine government to adopt significant trade liberalization measures during the early 1980s. These loans are expected to help ease some bottlenecks on the supply side for domestic industries, including the need for technology upgrading. This should enable those industries to benefit from the policy reforms which are designed to move towards a more liberalized trade regime. It is to be hoped that policy actions to deal with the country's immediate problems of debt servicing and foreign exchange will not significantly reduce the prospects of eventual trade liberalization and economic recovery.

The influence of the IMF in Philippine policy making will also be strongly felt, given its critical role in the debt-rescheduling negotiations between the government and foreign bank lenders. The IMF standby facility is pivotal, not so much for the funds it supplies as for the policy measures and quantitative targets in the economic programme which the Philippine government will be committed to adopt. The IMF standby agreements invariably emphasize monetary and fiscal tightness in order to restrain expenditures. They also usually involve an 'understanding' between the government of the debtor country and the Fund on exchange rate policy, including a substantial currency devaluation (in nominal terms). These measures can have severe implications for economic growth and income distribution in the short to medium term.

Contractionary monetary policies will raise domestic interest rates and reduce domestic bank lending, making it difficult for local firms to respond to market opportunities. Multinational companies will have an advantage in this situation to the extent that they can bring in foreign capital. Government budgetary controls will also serve to dampen economic activity in the short run. It is possible that an improvement in the quality of government expenditure may result from the reduction in volume, which would have salutary long-term effects. Also as already mentioned, there is considerable scope for increasing the efficiency of domestic investments, and austerity measures may spur local entrepreneurs (both public and private) to exploit such opportunities. Political factors as well as economic incentives (such as those associated with a more liberalized trade regime) will determine the extent to which existing and new investments can be made more efficient.

A decline in economic activity brought about by expenditure-reducing policies will, of course, reduce imports and further depress production in import-dependent industries. It can also affect exports. Given the high degree of import dependence of Philippine manufacturing industries (even those that are export-oriented), indigenous resource-based exports are more likely to contribute to the required adjustment in the trade balance and this will have a tendency to redirect income flows from urban to rural areas.

The resources released by a restructuring of aggregate demand through reductions in the government deficit and in the disposable income of affected households can be shifted to the production of exports and import substitutes, together defined as 'tradeable goods', through a change in incentives. That change is a devaluation in the real exchange rate which is the relative price of tradeable goods as a whole to that of non-tradeable goods as a whole.[17] Unless such an improvement in relative incentives and in the international competitiveness necessary for export expansion is achieved, it will not be possible to balance the current account and to sustain economic growth.

Thus for a nominal devaluation to result in a real devaluation a decline in the relative price of non-tradeables is essential. Where the production of non-tradeables is relatively labour-intensive, as is typical in developing countries, this would imply that real wages will have to fall, adversely affecting the economic welfare of common labourers. Since they are already at the bottom end of the income scale, this represents an unfavourable redistributive effect which will add to existing social and political problems. Direct measures to alleviate poverty might then need to be undertaken by the government.

The degree of adjustment necessary to put the balance of payments in order will be conditioned, as pointed out earlier, by the terms of debt repayments to be negotiated by the Philippines and foreign bank creditors, as well as by exogenous developments in the international economic environment, such as the growth of foreign demand for Philippine exports, terms of trade movements, behaviour of interest rates, and so on. If debt repudiation is to be avoided, the economic and political costs of coping with the debt service and balance-of-payments difficulties need to be minimized. International organizations such as the GATT, the IMF, and the World Bank can help by working to improve the conditions of world trade and payments and by exerting political leverage on foreign bank creditors to lessen the burden of adjustment through concessionary debt repayment terms. The more restrictive are the required adjustment policies, the greater is the risk of further aggravating political instability and the chances that the IMF performance criteria and debt service obligations will not be met.

NOTES AND REFERENCES

1. Jurado *et al.*, *op. cit.*, p. 106.

2. Linda M. Gard and James Riedel, 'Safeguard Protection of Industry in Developed Countries', *Weltwirtschaftliches Archiv*, Kiel, Vol. 116, No. 3, 1980.

3. About three-fifths of Philippine exports have gone to these two countries in the last decade or so. No other single country took more than 5 per cent of Philippine export trade during that period.

4. As reported in the *Far Eastern Economic Review*, Hong Kong, November 1984, p. 74.

5. For a detailed discussion, see Martin Wolf, 'Managed Trade in Practice: Implications for the Textile Arrangements', in William

R. Cline (ed.), *Trade Policy in the 1980s* (Washington: Institute for International Economics, 1983).

6. Quoted from the *Asian Wall Street Journal*, Hong Kong, 28 January 1982.

7. Alexander J. Yeats, *Trade Barriers Facing Developing Countries* (New York: St. Martins Press, 1979).

8. The Asian NICs are Singapore, Hong Kong, Republic of Korea and Taiwan. Near-NICs include Thailand, Malaysia, Indonesia and the Philippines. The ASEAN comprises Malaysia, Thailand, Singapore, Indonesia and the Philippines.

9. Isiah Frank, 'Trade Policy for the Developing Countries in the 1980s', Staff Working Paper No. 478 (Washington: World Bank, 1981).

10. Imports of ASEAN countries (except Singapore) have mainly concentrated on producer goods, especially capital equipment. The fact that the export structure of the NICs has been shifting to machinery and equipment in recent years implies a potential for expanded exports of such industrial products to the ASEAN countries.

11. Bautista, *Industrial Policy and Development in the ASEAN Countries*, Monograph Series No. 2 (Manila: Philippine Institute for Development Studies, 1983).

12. Kym Anderson, 'Economic Development, Changing Comparative Advantage, and Food Trade: Pacific Basin Experience', paper presented at the Second Western Pacific Food Trade Workshop, Jakarta, 22-23 August 1982.

13. One of the early supporters of this view is Martin Feldstein, former Chairman of the United States President's Council of Economic Advisors; see *The Washington Post*, Washington, 9 May 1984.

14. *The Economist*, London, 27 October 1984, p. 91.

15. Cline, 'Introduction and Summary', in Cline (ed.), *op. cit.*, p. 14.

16. Quoted from the *Far Eastern Economic Review*, Hong Kong, 18 October 1984. Under the Subsidies Code, petitions for countervailing duties need to pass an 'injury test', a process so cumbersome that petitioners eventually lose interest.

17. From an economic point of view the distinction between a tradeable and a non-tradeable commodity (or service) is that the price of the former is set by the price in world trade (adjusted by the exchange rate and any tariffs, subsidies or sales taxes). The price

of tradeables is unaffected by domestic demand. The prices of non-tradeables, however, are determined by the interplay of domestic supply and demand. It follows that when an import-competing product is protected by a binding quantitative restriction, it becomes a non-tradeable product in economic terms.

Chapter 6

Hope for Future Trade Liberalization

CONSISTENT with President Aquino's democratic zeal, the new government appears committed (at least on paper) to a greater reliance on market forces and private initiative which withered under the previous regime's 'crony capitalism' that conferred illicit economic gains on close friends and relatives of the Marcos family. Also, the long-standing neglect of, and effective discrimination against, the agricultural sector are to be rectified. In a report of the National Economic and Development authority, *Agenda for People-powered Development*, which was approved by the Cabinet in October 1986, two major policy directions are indicated: (i) correction of price biases against agricultural products and (ii) raising farm productivity through increased public investment in rural infrastructure. One of the key elements of an 'agriculture-based development strategy' is a liberalized foreign trade regime.

Economic Policies under the Aquino Government

The strategic role being given to the agricultural and rural sectors seems well placed, considering that the Philippine economy is still heavily agricultural;[1] fully two-thirds of the country's population are in the rural areas where agriculture and related production activities represent, almost by definition, the principal means of livelihood. Raising rural incomes by means of increased agricultural prices and productivity is expected to provide the initial stimulus, through final demand effects, to a more rapid growth of the national economy. This is based on the recognition of the high marginal propensity of rural households to buy food and other labour-intensive consumer goods. Hence, it is to be expected that a given increase in rural income will generate large income and employment multiplier effects. On the supply side, an agriculture-based development process is also attractive, given the existing foreign exchange shortage in the Philippines, because of the lower import requirements of agricultural production relative to the encouragement of the more import-dependent and capital-intensive industrial sector. Finally, in a country where the rural-urban income differential is quite large,[2] rising employment and income in the rural areas may well prove to be the most efficient means of improving income distribution — which is of major policy concern in the Philippines.

The Marcos regime left a legacy of heavy taxation on agricultural products not only in terms of direct export taxes but also, and more importantly, by the implicit taxation of agriculture through currency over-valuation due to trade restrictions and balance-of-payments disequilibrium. The price biases against agricultural products translate into an effective resource transfer out of the agricultural sector that is quite large relative to the amount of resource transfer into agriculture from government spending. In 1980, for example, the latter was about $460 million; by comparison, even considering export crop agriculture only, the resource outflow amounted to $868 million, consisting of $303 million from explicit export taxes and $560 million from policy-induced exchange rate over-valuation.[3]

The Aquino Government has abolished export taxes and dismantled the agricultural trade monopolies headed by the 'crony capitalists' of the previous regime. Price supports for rice and corn have also been maintained in the face of temporarily low world cereal prices. All this will help to prevent a decline in the agricultural terms of trade such as occurred during the second half of the 1970s and early 1980s.

The other means of raising rural income being implemented by the new government involves the marked expansion of public investment in the rural areas. The government's expenditure programme has placed heavy emphasis on employment-generating rural infrastructure projects, aimed at creating one million jobs annually in the first few years. Two mechanisms will be at work, tending to improve the real purchasing power of rural households: (i) the increased government spending will have an immediate positive effect on rural employment and income and (ii) rural infrastructure development will help increase agricultural productivity over time, sustaining the growth of rural income. Through this programme and its employment and income multiplier effects, the low income labouring classes will participate in a demand-driven, long-run expansion of the country's productive capacity.

Whether supply will be able to match the increased demand by the rural population for those products will depend on the availability of production inputs and their prices. Thus, if intermediate inputs to agricultural and non-agricultural production are made artificially scarce or expensive by a restrictive foreign trade regime, the full benefits from the final demand effects in terms of output growth and labour absorption will not be realized. It is also clear that public investment in infrastructure is critical not only for the generation and diffusion of new technologies but also for the development and integration of rural markets. It will serve to increase the responsiveness of supply to price incentives, enhancing the long-run effectiveness of reform in trade and exchange rate policies.

Because of the high degree of tradeability of agricultural output in the Philippines, the exchange rate exerts a significant influence on the domestic prices of agricultural products. It has been estimated, for example, that exchange rate over-valuation effectively lowered the domestic agricultural price relative to non-tradeable goods by 19 per cent and relative to non-agricultural products by 25 per cent during the period

1975-80.[4] To prevent the exchange rate from being overvalued, it will be necessary to reduce or abandon import restrictions which protect domestic industry while at the same time maintaining a sustainable trade balance. A more realistic exchange rate policy would encourage, in the long run, not only export production but also efficient import substitution in the agricultural sector as well as in the rest of the economy.

The importance of a liberalized trade regime for sustained long-run growth of the Philippine economy is not being questioned by policy makers in the Aquino Government. The apprehension about import liberalization frequently expressed since the economic crisis began in late 1983 is that, given the country's under-utilized production capacity caused by the IMF-imposed expenditure reduction,[5] exposure to foreign competition will inhibit domestic producers from utilizing excess capacity and expanding output. On the other hand, continuing import restrictions and distorted relative pricing give the wrong signal to private investors. An appropriate approach to this policy dilemma would be to reduce tariff and non-tariff barriers gradually during the economic recovery period; the government should also make clear at an early stage its commitment to a trade regime of low and uniform protection rates across production sectors. This will help to prevent the misuse of existing capital and the inefficient allocation of new investment. At the same time, direct subsidies can be provided temporarily to producers whose installed capital could be more fully utilized in a socially optimal manner, that is, when the net social benefit (based on shadow prices) exceeds private profitability.

Under the new government's import liberalization scheme, developed in consultation with the IMF and the World Bank, 1,232 import items will be removed from various controls between April 1986 and May 1988. In November 1986, only 303 products were still covered by quantitative restrictions (quotas, import licensing or outright bans), consisting of 180 intermediate and capital goods, 101 raw materials and 22 consumer goods. Tariff rates of up to 50 per cent have been imposed on the 929 import items on which the quantitative restrictions were lifted, such tariff rates being planned to be gradually adjusted to a uniform low level over a five-year period.[6] It is to be hoped that a clear signal has been made by the government that it will not waver from the commitment to a liberalized trade regime and that the investment behaviour of domestic producers will be guided by the long-run message of a uniform low tariff system.

Other aspects of domestic policy will need to be supportive of the development strategy being adopted. Encouragement to small and medium-scale industrial producers in the rural areas is warranted to enable them to fulfil their productive potential. Compared to large urban producers, they are likely to be more efficient producers of many industrial consumer goods and services for which demand is expected to rise significantly with the increase in rural income because their transportation and marketing costs will be lower. In contrast to the past pattern of urban-oriented, regionally concentrated, capital-intensive and large-scale industrialization, what is needed to complement the growth in agricultural output and rural income would be a rural-based, regionally dispersed, labour-intensive and small-scale development of the manufacturing sector. It can also be expected that a structure of industrial growth of this kind will lead to less import-dependence because intermediate inputs will be more likely to be sourced locally. The past government's lip service to regional dispersal of industry and promotion of small and medium-scale industries should now be transformed into effective action, for example, through substantial improvements in transportation, communication, electrification and credit facilities supportive of small industry development in the rural areas.

Technical and financial assistance for the rationalization of existing industries should not only be continued as planned but expanded beyond the list of industries already identified. The need to redirect production more efficiently within particular industries is more acutely felt by the producers themselves than by government bureaucrats. Limiting the potential beneficiaries of the industrial revitalization programme is therefore unwarranted; it would only reduce the number of domestic producers that can position themselves to take advantage of the eventual recovery of both the domestic and export markets. It is particularly important during the economic recovery period to protect the trade balance — to which an internationally competitive domestic industry can significantly contribute.

New industrial investments in the form of large-scale capital-intensive projects need to be evaluated very carefully before active encouragement is given by the government. In view of some glaring inefficiencies in past investments promoted by the government, greater reliance on private initiative in the formulation and implementation of large industrial projects is called for. Any existing bias in the protective tariff and tax structure against intermediate and capital goods-producing sectors should be dealt with in the most direct and comprehensive manner, namely, through policy reforms in tariffs and indirect taxes.

The previous government's efforts to offset domestic price distortions caused by trade and exchange rate policies by giving fiscal and other incentives to 'priority' investments (administered by the Board of Investments) did not succeed because of the high degree of selectivity in the granting of such incentives. Inevitably the priority areas were determined by the BOI on a narrow basis, given its limited administrative capacity; moreover, the system of BOI incentives failed to reach the small producers. A good case can be made, therefore, for the phasing out of BOI incentives as the structure of protection becomes more uniform with adoption of trade liberalization measures.

On the same grounds export promotion should be made general rather than selective. The past practice of the Ministry of Trade and Industry to signal out 'specific priority exports ... on the basis of their recent growth, the increasing demand facing them, and their potential in utilizing the country's comparative advantage'[7] is harmful to the extent that other industries, for which the promotional measures (provision of market information, export infrastructure development and so on) may have higher present and future payoffs, are being excluded. Again, the relevant question is: are government bureaucrats able to predict which industries will become successful exporters?

The External Economic Environment

As pointed out earlier the desirability of trade liberalization and other improvements in domestic policy does not depend on what may or may not happen in the external economic environment. It is also true, however, that more favourable external developments will imply greater opportunities for the domestic economy to gain from trade.

Since the mid-1970s there has been a discernible rise in the incidence of trade restrictions, especially non-tariff barriers, in the markets of developed countries. The protectionist measures have been particularly strong against agricultural commodities and labour-intensive manufactured goods, product categories which are of major export interest to the Philippines. Moreover, bilateral and regional trading arrangements have increased, restricting the trade of third countries; such arrangements are also in contravention of the GATT rules. The responses of developing countries have likewise departed from the basic GATT principle of non-discrimination, accentuating recent tendencies towards sectoralism, bilateralism and regionalism.

Governments of both developed and developing countries can help restore confidence in the open trading system by displaying a greater willingness to adhere to the GATT rules and principles. The declaration of a standstill on new trade barriers by the major signatories of the GATT which occurred in the Punta del Este declaration of September 1986 launching the Uruguay round of negotiations in the GATT, will be a useful first step, if it turns out to be effective. In the course of the Uruguay round a rollback of existing trade restrictions and discriminatory practices in both developed and developing countries should begin; this was also agreed at Punta del Este. The GATT settlement procedures also need to be respected rather than 'corrupted', especially by the major trading countries.[8]

The Philippines and other ASEAN countries would be particularly interested in having the GATT rules extended to trade in agriculture, textiles and other labour-intensive manufactures and resource-intensive goods. More specifically, this would involve the phasing out of the European Community's common agricultural policy, the MFA and tariff escalation in developed countries on processed primary products. Significant gains in this direction would encourage reciprocal moves by the developing countries toward liberalization of their own foreign trade regimes.

Failing multilateral trade liberalization, the next best hope is for like-minded countries to make a global contribution by lowering trade barriers through regional cooperation. This would naturally involve products of export interest to the participating countries but should not discriminate against countries outside the region. It has been cogently argued that countries in the Asian-Pacific region, representing the world's most dynamic areas, are in the best position to provide such a contribution towards the strengthening of the multilateral trading system and to become a force within the GATT for global trade liberalization.[9] As discussed earlier, the Philippines would benefit from import liberalization in several Pacific Basin countries where market access continues to be restrictive with respect to labour-intensive manufactured products.

Based on the record of the ASEAN contries, sub-regional trading arrangements within the Asian-Pacific region are more likely to discriminate against third countries. They could, however, also serve as a political force towards equalization of trading opportunities. Following the example of the United States and the European Community, ASEAN countries would be well-advised to mount their own political lobbying for the lowering of import barriers in Japan on products of export interest to them. Apparently motivated by the need to overcome the increasing threat of protectionism against Japanese exports because of the inaccessibility of its own market, official measures have been taken in Japan to boost imports from the United States and European Community. Joint efforts of ASEAN countries in seeking trade concessions from Japan would, of course, be more effective than individual country efforts. The political clout of the ASEAN countries together would be a clear case of the whole being greater than the sum of its parts.

Because of the debt service and foreign exchange difficulties faced by the Philippines, there is a great deal of domestic resistance to meaningful trade liberalization, as will be discussed in the next section. The government's clear commitment to a liberalized trade regime together with some supporting policy actions as indicated above, need to be made. The influence of the World Bank in the formulation and implementation of some of these policies will be felt as the succeeding structural adjustment loans to the Philippines are negotiated and disbursed. On the basis of the earlier discussion, much can be done in dealing with problems of micro-economic inefficiency, in both the agricultural and industrial sectors. The increased political leverage of the World Bank can be put to good use. Structural adjustment policies that improve the allocation and utilization of existing and new investments are clearly needed.

The terms of IMF conditionality related to the $615 million SDRs standby loan, as well as the repayment terms of rescheduled debt with foreign bank creditors, will undoubtedly have a bearing on the prospects of the Philippine economy in the medium term and on whether the government's commitment to policy reforms will be sustained. Some budgetary control and monetary stability are, of course, needed for the resumption of stable growth. The economic and political difficulties associated with extreme measures of austerity, however, may render the IMF performance criteria self-defeating. Drastically curtailing imports through expenditure reduction would, indeed, improve the trade balance but the repercussions on output and employment could be so severe, as shown by the 1984-85 experience, as to generate domestic political pressures for the government to retreat from its policy commitments to the IMF. Alternatively, some scope for economic growth should be provided by assuring adequate credit to deserving industries, in particular export-oriented producers using mainly indigenous raw materials. This would not only stimulate domestic production and labour absorption but would also promote efficient balance of payments adjustment through export expansion; it would also help to ensure that the country would continue to have the ability to service its external debt.

In the same vein, making the terms of debt repayments excessively stringent runs the risk of the Philippines eventually failing to meet its debt service obligations. Clearly, stable growth of the Philippine economy is also in the long-term interest of foreign bank creditors. 'Stretching out' the short-term debt of the less developed countries into 20-30 year loans at concessionary interest rates would undoubtedly ease domestic economic and political pressures, improving the prospects for sustained economic growth and loan repayments.

Finally, it would be desirable to incorporate in debt repayment agreements with foreign bank creditors, an automatic adjustment in the payments schedule to accommodate external shocks such as a sharp deterioration of a country's terms of trade or an upward movement in interest rates. In this connection, there is good reason to apply a ceiling on the proportion of foreign exchange earnings that can be used in any given year for debt servicing.

Stabilization policy targets and performance criteria determined by the IMF also need to be made flexible so that they can be adjusted quickly when the country is hit by forces beyond its control. Lack of such flexibility in the terms of IMF conditionality underlying the standby loan, as well as the debt rescheduling agreement with the foreign bank creditors, will only add to uncertainty about the eventual resolution of the debt servicing and foreign exchange problems of the Philippines. It will also make more difficult the early adoption of trade liberalization and other measures that can help improve micro-economic efficiency and sustain the country's general economic performance.

Impediments to and Prospects for Trade Liberalization

The preceding section has emphasized the influence of international economic conditions on the prospects for trade liberalization in the Philippines. It does not assume that such external factors are wholly exogenous. Although nothing can be done to avoid deteriorating terms of trade or rising interests rates, the government can (and should) negotiate with the IMF for a less severe macro-economic adjustment programme and with the commercial bank creditors for debt rescheduling on concessionary terms. Highly austere macro-economic policies, such as those adopted during 1984-85 at the insistence of the IMF, are not only self-defeating because of the impaired capacity to sustain any improvement in the balance of payments, but also politically risky in view of the heavy burden of adjustment falling on low-income groups. It is hardly a coincidence that the Communist insurgency movement has expanded rapidly since the early 1980s, particularly so in the regions hard hit by the economic recession. The conduct of macro-economic policy should take into account the country's need for rapid economic recovery which requires that the government be more assertive of its sovereignty in domestic policy making.

With respect to the negotiations with foreign bank creditors, the Aquino Government should take advantage of the country's improved creditworthiness and strong international support to seek liberal debt rescheduling terms. By the end of 1986 Philippine negotiators had been unable to obtain from the bank negotiating committee (representing the biggest bank lenders, mostly American) the concessionary terms that Mexico received earlier, perhaps indicating the greater political importance of the latter country to the United States.[10] In any case, patience and determination by the government with support, it is hoped, from the IMF and World Bank, can only lead to a more favourable debt rescheduling arrangement with the bank creditors. It is clear, however, that a resolution of the debt-service problem is necessary for a continued implementation of trade liberalization measures.

On the domestic front, impediments to trade liberalization remain substantial. As discussed in Chapter 4 the country's political and economic problems are inextricably intertwined. It would be unreasonable to expect that the new government's economic reform programme will not be met by political opposition, which can arise from within and outside the government. A frequent commentary among cynical observers is that the February 1986 revolution has not brought into power a new ruling class. Economic corruption is not going to disappear overnight.[11] Good intentions at the top can be frustrated by the promotion of personal and family interests at lower levels of government; this partly explains the replacement of some prominent senior officials within a short period in office of the new government. Since the opportunities for rent-seeking are reduced by economic liberalization, it can be expected that there will be efforts within the government to resist the movement toward freer foreign trade.

During the Marcos era, senior technocrats in the Cabinet championed the cause of economic liberalization placing themselves, for example, on the side of the minority group of non-traditional export producers that were being discriminated against by the trade and exchange rate policies then in existence. The technocrats were most effective during the first half of the 1970s after which their influence weakened as President Marcos increasingly felt the need to promote the economic interest of 'crony capitalists'. Discredited by their association with the Marcos regime, minister-technocrats are relatively absent in the new government, Cabinet members having been chosen seemingly on the basis of their contribution to bringing Mrs Aquino to power. A few key officials are known to be associated with business interests (for example, in some heavily protected industries producing import sustitutes) that stand to lose from a policy reform towards a more open trade regime. Left-wing officials in the Aquino Government who want more government control over the economy, present another threat to trade liberalization. If such sources of conflict are not removed, there is reason to be sceptical that a genuine commitment to trade liberalization can be made. Government policy pronouncements can always be issued to suit the international audience; appearances, however, may not reflect reality.

Outside the government, opposition to a liberalized trade regime comes from producer interests in the affected industries, that is, those faced with significant reductions in effective protection. They are more powerful, economically and politically, than other producer groups and consumer interests in general. The latter are not well organized and are largely unaware of the potential gains from trade liberalization. Also, self-promoted 'economic nationalists' have long been naively arguing for the protection of any and all domestic industries against foreign competition. They do not realize that protecting one industry effectively means penalizing another; they wrongly assume that protected infant industries will grow efficiently into maturity. They also do not acknowledge the social costs of such protection to consumers, especially the low-income families, in terms of the induced high prices and low product quality and to workers who remain less than fully employed because of the resulting inefficiency with which resources are being allocated and used. Some such economic nationalists are ideologues who have taken an extreme reaction to past colonial rule and to whom anything foreign is anathema to national development. Others, and the more vociferous, have personal and family interest in promoting particular industries.

The 'true' economic nationalists are sometimes said to be those who have taken up arms and are waging a violent campaign against the social injustices of the 'system'. Whether ideology or poverty has been the primary motivation for the rank-and-file of the Communist insurgency movement is an open question. To the extent that domestic market distortions caused by trade and exchange rate policies have contributed to economic deprivation for some segments of the population, policy reform towards a more open trade regime may contribute to the reduction of social tensions.

Prospects for trade liberalization can be improved significantly if public opinion is informed of the heavy cost of protecting sectoral interests and subsidizing inefficient industries. In retrospect, Philippine policy makers have not given due attention to this function. The failure to educate the general public on the consequences of alternative trade policies might well have been the underlying reason for of the inward-looking development strategy pursued throughout most of the post-World War II period. This is all the more unfortunate considering that the costs of protection have been well documented by academic researchers, as can be seen from the discussion in Chapter 2.

There is reasonable hope for trade liberalization in the Philippines if the government makes a determined effort to improve public understanding of the value of foreign trade to economic growth and the critical importance of liberal trade policies in promoting the international competitiveness of domestic industries and the overall efficiency of the national economy. This will provide a base on which to build a political consensus that will facilitate the resolution of the various sources of conflict indicated above in any sustained drive towards trade liberalization.

NOTES AND REFERENCES

1. The agricultural sector contributes directly and indirectly about two-thirds of total employment and one-half of the country's gross domestic product. Also, it earns some 40 per cent of total export receipts (from raw and simply processed agricultural products), while agricultural imports account for less than 10 per

cent of the total import bill.

2. In the early 1980s the average income of rural households in the Philippines was only one-half that of urban households.

3. See Chapter 8 in Bautista, *Effects of Trade and Exchange Rate Policies*, *op. cit.*

4. *Ibid.*, Ch. 7.

5. As already indicated, real GNP decreased absolutely by nearly 10 per cent in the two year period 1984-85.

6. By the end of 1986 no exact indication of the eventual level of uniform tariff had been officially given although 10 to 30 per cent rates have been mentioned in policy discussions.

7. Gwendolyn R. Tecson, 'Trade and Promotion Policy in Philippine Industrial Development', *The Developing Economies*, December 1983, p. 408.

8. For details of how various tactics undermining the integrity of the GATT settlement procedures are employed, see Lydia Dunn *et al.*, *In the Kingdom of the Blind: a Report on Protectionism and the Asian-Pacific Region*, Special Report No. 3 (London: Trade Policy Research Centre, 1983) p. 77.

9. *Ibid.*, Ch. 5.

10. Indeed, the much publicized Bradley proposal for easing the debt-service problem for major debtor countries, which has a 'partial loan forgiveness' component, is directed only to the Latin American countries.

11. For a detailed discussion of economic corruption as 'a vital feature of the economy' see Florian Alburo and Geoffrey Shepherd, 'Trade Liberalization: the Philippine Experience', mimeograph, Philippine Institute for Development Studies, May 1986, p. 26 and Sicat, *A Historical and Current Perspective of Philippine Economic Problems*, Monograph Series No. 11 (Manila: Philippine Institute for Development Studies, 1986) for illustrative cases.

List of References

THIS list contains only the more important references cited in the text. The reader should refer to the Notes and References at the end of each chapter for more complete bibliographical information.

ROBERT E. BALDWIN, *Foreign Trade Regimes and Economic Development: The Philippines* (New York: National Bureau of Economic Research, 1975).

JAGDISH N. BHAGWATI and T.N. SCRINIVASAN, 'Trade Policy and Development', in Rudiger Dornbush and Jacob Frenkel (eds), *International Economic Policy: Theory and Evidence* (Baltimore: Johns Hopkins Press, 1978).

ROMEO M. BAUTISTA, *Production Incentives in Philippine Agriculture: Effects of Trade and Exchange Rate Policies*, Research Report No. 59 (Washington: International Food Policy Research Institute, 1987).

ROMEO M. BAUTISTA, 'Structural Change in the Philippines', in B. Krause and Sueo Sekiguchi (eds), *Economic Interaction in the Pacific Basin* (Washington: Brookings Institution, 1980).

LYDIA DUNN *et. al.*, *In the Kingdom of the Blind: a Report on Protectionism and the Asian-Pacific Region*, Special Report No. 3 (London: Trade Policy Research Centre, 1983).

CRAIG EMERSON and PETER G. WARR, 'Economic Evaluation of Mineral Processing Projects: a Case Study of Copper

Smelting in the Philippines', *Philippine Economic Journal*, Manila, Vol. XX, No. 2, 1981.

LINDA M. GARD and JAMES RIEDEL, 'Safeguard Protection of Industry in Developed Countires', *Weltwirtschaftliches Archiv*, Kiel, Vol. 116, No. 3, 1980.

HELEN HUGHES, 'External Debt Problems of Developing Countries', in Bautista and Saja Naya (eds), *Energy and Structural Change in the Asia-Pacific Region* (Manila: Philippine Institute for Development Studies and Asian Development Bank, 1984).

Sharing in Development in the Philippines (Geneva: International Labour Office, 1974).

MAHAR MANGAHAS and BRUNO BARROS, *The Distribution of Income and Wealth: a Survey on Philippine Research*, School of Economics Discussion Paper 7916 (Manila: University of the Philippines, 1979).

Five-year Philippine Development Plan, 1978-1982 (updated for 1981 and 1982) (Manila: National Economic Development Authority).

Tariff Profiles in ASEAN (Manila: National Economic and Development Authority, for the Trade Commission, 1979).

JOHN H. POWER, *Response of Payments Crisis in the 1970s: Korea and the Philippines*, Staff Working Paper No. 83-05 (Manila: Philippine Institute for Development Studies, 1983).

JOHN H. POWER and GERARDO P. SICAT, *The Philippines: Industrialisation and Trade Policies* (London: Oxford University Press, 1971).

NORMA A. TAN, 'The Structure of Protection and Resource Flows in the Philippines', in Bautista, Power and Associates, *Industrial Promotion Policies in the Philippines* (Manila: Philippine Institute for Development Studies, 1979).

ROSALINDA P. TIDALGO and EMMANUEL F. ESGUERRA, *Philippine*

Employment in the Seventies (Manila: Philippine Institute for Development Studies, 1984).

MARTIN WOLF, 'Managed Trade in Practise: Implications for the Textile Arrangements', in William R. Cline (ed.), *Trade Policy in the 1980s* (Washington: Institute for International Economics, 1983).

The Philippines: Development Problems and Prospects (Washington: Johns Hopkins Press, for the World Bank, 1976).

ALEXANDER J. YEATS, *Trade Barriers Facing Developing Countries* (New York: St. Martins Press, 1979).

Participation Studies Programme

AS PART of the Trade Policy Research Centre's programme of studies on the Participation of Developing Countries in the International Trading System, three general studies have been published, focussing on economic and legal issues in the GATT system *per se*.

Myths and Reality of External Constraints on Development, by James Riedel, of Johns Hopkins University's School of Advanced International Studies in Washington, questions the widely-held belief that conditions in developed countries determine the growth of exports from, and the availability of capital to, developing countries. To free themselves from this perceived 'external constraint', many developing countries have insisted on the need to pursue industrialization through import-substitution policies, on their need to borrow on concessional terms and on their need to be accorded preferential access to developed-country markets.

Professor Riedel argues that there is now a genuine alternative to these policies and demands for special privileges. With developing countries diversifying their exports and moving into the production of industrial products, they can now seek more secure access to the markets of developed countries, provided that they can retain their competitiveness. Similarly, he examines the implications of developing countries receiving improved access to capital markets, particularly the opportunities this development makes. Much depends though on their own domestic policies in promoting economic development.

Economic Impact of Generalized Tariff Preferences, by Rolf J. Langhammer, a Senior Research Fellow at the Institut für Weltwirtschaft, Kiel, and André Sapir, Professor of Economics at the Free University of Brussels, analyzes the effects of the schemes under the Generalized System of Preferences (GSP) that are operated by the European Community and the United States. The GSP is a formal derogation from the principle of non-discrimination, the cornerstone of the GATT. Developing countries have contested the principle of non-discrimination and the GSP has come to symbolize their demands for 'special and more favourable treatment' of their exports of manufactures and semi-manufactures to developed countries.

There is little evidence, the authors conclude, that preferences are effective in stimulating developing-country exports. Indeed, the way those preferences are administered reflects an overall protectionist tendency in developed-country trade policies, especially discrimination against successful developing-country exporters.

Developing countries need to focus on the liberalization of non-tariff measures and on general tariff liberalization. The more advanced, in particular, would be better advised to participate in the reciprocal bargaining process of the Uruguay Round negotiations now proceeding in Geneva rather than insist on their continued eligibility for tariff preferences.

Developing Countries in the GATT Legal System, by Robert E. Hudec, Steen Professor of Law at the University of Minnesota, traces the evolution of the GATT's current legal policy towards developing countries, detailing the successive departures from GATT obligations to satisfy demands for 'special and differential treatment'. In a growing conflict over the role developing countries should play in the international trading system, developed countries are calling on developing countries to assume fuller participation in legal disciplines of the GATT. Professor Hudec questions the assumption that fuller legal participation by developing countries will bring about greater access to developed-country markets, but it will enable developing countries to achieve better internal control over their own trade policies, he argues.

The study concludes that the GATT's current legal policy has failed to serve the interests of its developing-country members and ends by proposing several policy initiatives to begin the long and difficult task of reversing that policy.

List of Thames Essays

OCCASIONAL papers of the Trade Policy Research Centre are published under the omnibus heading of Thames Essays. Set out below are the particulars of those published to date. The first 44 titles were published under the Centre's sole imprint, but they may also be obtained from the Gower Publishing Company, its addresses in the United Kingdom, the United States of America and Australia being set out in the reverse of the title page of this essay.

1 GERARD and VICTORIA CURZON, *Hidden Barriers to International Trade* (1970), 75 pp.

2 T.E. JOSLING, *Agriculture and Britain's Trade Policy Dilemma* (1970), 52 pp.

3 GERARD and VICTORIA CURZON, *Global Assault on Non-tariff Trade Barriers* (1972), 44 pp.

4 BRIAN HINDLEY, *Britain's Position on Non-tariff Protection* (1972), 60 pp.

5 GEOFFREY DENTON and SEAMUS O'CLEIREACAIN, *Subsidy Issues in International Commerce* (1972), 75 pp.

6 GEORGE F. RAY, *Western Europe and the Energy Crisis* (1975), 68 pp.

7 THEODORE GEIGER, JOHN VOLPE and ERNEST H. PREEG, *North American Integration and Economic Blocs* (1975), 65 pp.

8 Hugh Corbet, W.M. Corden, Brian Hindley, Roy Batchelor and Patrick Minford, *On How to Cope with Britain's Trade Position* (1977), 80 pp.

9 Peter Lloyd, *Anti-dumping Actions and the GATT System* (1977), 59 pp.

10 T.E. Josling, *Agriculture in the Tokyo Round Negotiations* (1977), 48 pp.

11 Harald B. Malmgren, *International Order for Public Subsidies* (1977), 80 pp.

12 David Robertson, *Fail Safe Systems for Trade Liberalisation* (1977), 80 pp.

13 Sidney Golt, *Developing Countries in the GATT System* (1978), 42 pp.

14 Theodore Heidhues, T.E. Josling, Christopher Ritson and Stefan Tangermann, *Common Prices and Europe's Farm Policy* (1978), 83 pp.

15 Hans Böhme, *Restraints on Competition in World Shipping* (1978), 92 pp.

16 Robert E. Hudec, *Adjudication of International Trade Disputes* (1978), 95 pp.

17 Stuart Harris, Mark Salmon and Ben Smith, *Analysis of Commodity Markets for Policy Purposes* (1978), 91 pp.

18 Robert Z. Aliber, *Stabilising World Monetary Arrangements* (1979), 51 pp.

19 Robert L. Carter and Gerard M. Dickinson, *Barriers to Trade in Insurance* (1979), *Out of Print.*

20 Geoffrey Smith, *Westminster Reform: Learning from Congress* (1979), 59 pp.

21 W.M. Corden, *The NIEO Proposals: a Cool Look* (1979), *Out of Print.*

22 Robert E. Baldwin, *Beyond the Tokyo Round Negotiations* (1979), 46 pp.

23 Donald B. Keesing and Martin Wolf, *Textile Quotas against Developing Countries* (1980), 226 pp.

24 M.FG. Scott, W.M. Corden and I.M.D. Little, *The Case against General Import Restrictions* (1980), 107 pp.

25 Victoria Curzon Price, *Unemployment and Other Non-work Issues* (1980), 63 pp.

26 V.N. Balasubramanyam, *Multinational Enterprises and the Third World* (1980), 89 pp.

27 T.E. Josling, Mark Langworthy and Scott Pearson, *Options for Farm Policy in the European Community* (1981), 96 pp.

28 Deepak Lal, *Resurrection of the Pauper-labour Argument* (1981), 82 pp.

29 Isaiah Frank, *Trade Policy Issues of Interest to the Third World* (1981), 76 pp.

30 Geoffrey Shepherd, *Textile-industry Adjustment in Developed Countries* (1981), 68 pp.

31 Charles Collyns, *Can Protection Cure Unemployment?* (1982), 95 pp.

32 Brian Hindley, *Economic Analysis and Insurance Policy in the Third World* (1982), 68 pp.

33 Hugh Corbet, *Beyond the Rhetoric of Commodity Power*, second edition (forthcoming).

34 Brian Hindley and Eri Nicolaides, *Taking the New Protectionism Seriously* (1983), second edition forthcoming.

35 Kent Jones, *Impasse and Crisis in Steel Trade Policy* (1983), 108 pp.

36 Charles Pearson, *Emergency Protection in the Footwear Industry* (1983), 101 pp.

37 Martin Wolf, Hans Hinrich Glismann, Joseph Pelzman and Dean Spinanger, *Costs of Protecting Jobs in Textiles and Clothing* (1984), 163 pp.

38 José de la Torre, *Clothing-industry Adjustment in Developed Countries* (1984), 286 pp.

39 Kenneth W. Clements and Larry A. Sjaastad, *How Protection Taxes Exporters* (1984), 87 pp.

40 T.G. Congdon, *Economic Liberalism in the Cone of Latin America* (1985), 130 pp.

41 Ingo Walter, *Barriers to Trade in Banking and Financial Services* (1985), 136 pp.

42 Basil S. Yamey, Richard L. Sandor and Brian Hindley, *How Commodity Futures Markets Work* (1985), 80 pp.

43 David Greenaway and Brian Hindley, *What Britain Pays for Voluntary Export Restraints* (1985), 178 pp.

44 Elliot Schrier, Ernest Nadel and Bertram Rifas, *Outlook for the Liberalisation of Maritime Transport* (1985), 94 pp.

45 Gary Banks and Jan Tumlir, *Economic Policy and the Adjustment Problem* (1986), 101 pp.

46 Richard Pryke, *Competition among International Airlines* (1987), 113 pp.

47 James Riedel, *Myths and Reality of External Constraints on Development* (1987), 104 pp.

48 David Bevan, Arne Bigsten, Paul Collier and Jan Willem Gunning, *East African Lessons on Economic Liberalization* (1987), 72 pp.

49 Rolf J. Langhammer and André Sapir, *Economic Impact of Generalized Tariff Preferences* (1987), 89 pp.

50 Robert E. Hudec, *Developing Countries in the GATT Legal System* (1987), 255 pp.

51 Deepak Lal and Sarath Rajapatirana, *Impediments to Trade Liberalization in Sri Lanka* (1988), 67 pp.

52 Jimmye S. Hillman and Robert A. Rothenberg, *Agricultural Trade and Protection in Japan*, (1988) 96 pp.

53 J.P. Hayes, *Economic Effects of Sanctions on Southern Africa* (1987), 100 pp.

54 Romeo M. Bautista, *Impediments to Trade Liberalization in the Philippines*, (1988), 81 pp..

List of Special Reports

IN 1981 the Trade Policy Research Centre initiated a series of Special Reports, each the product of a study group concerned with clarifying major issues of the day in terms accessible to lay readers.

1 LORD MCFADZEAN of KELVINSIDE *et al.*, *Global Strategy for Growth: a Report on North-South Issues* (1981), 112 pp., prepared in response to the Report of the Independent Commission on International Development Issues, better known as the Brandt Report.

2 KENNETH DURHAM *et al.*, *Words Are Not Enough: a Report on the Perils of Protectionism*, in mimeograph (1982), prepared for a meeting of ministers, senior officials, business leaders and independent experts held at Ditchley Park, near Oxford, on 2-4 September 1982 (out of print).

3 LYDIA DUNN *et al.*, *In the Kingdom of the Blind: a Report on Protectionism and the Asian-Pacific Region* (1983), 159 pp., prepared for the first Asian-Pacific Trade Conference, held in Hobart on 25-27 March 1983, hosted by the Government of Australia. The report has also been published in Korean by the Korea Foreign Traders Association.

4 KENNETH DURHAM *et al.*, *Living in the Long Run: a Report on Inflation, Protectionism and Sovereign Debt*, in mimeograph (1983), prepared for a meeting of ministers, senior officials,

business leaders and independent experts at Leeds Castle, near Canterbury, on 14-16 July 1983 (out of print).

5 André Bénard *et al.*, *A Europe Open to the World: a Report on Protectionism and the European Community* (1984), 115 pp., prepared by a European task force sponsored by the Centre and the Associazione italiana per el Commercio mondiale in Milan, the Institut de l'Entreprise in Paris, the Institut de l'Enterprise (Belgique) in Brussels, the Institut der Deutschen Wirtschaft in Cologne and the Strichting Maatschappij en Onderneming in the Hague.

6 Brian Scott *et al.*, *Has the Cavalry Arrived? a Report on Trade Liberalisation and Economic Recovery* (1984), 156 pp., prepared for the second Asian-Pacific Trade Conference held in Seoul on 3-5 April 1984, hosted by the Government of Korea.

7 Olivier Long *et al.*, *Public Scrutiny of Protection: Domestic Policy Transparency and Trade Liberalization* (1988), 74 pp. Draft copies of the report were circulated in Geneva and the main proposals have already been taken up in the Uruguay Round's negotiating group on the functioning of the GATT system.

8 Nam Duck-Woo *et al.*, *When the Going Gets Tough: Need for Early Progress in the Uruguay Round* (forthcoming), prepared for the fourth Asian-Pacific Trade Conference, held in Bali on 8-10 January 1988, hosted by the Government of Indonesia.

The World Economy

THE Trade Policy Research Centre's quarterly journal, *The World Economy*, provides a continuous focus on the conduct of international economic affairs. Published for the Centre by Basil Blackwell, based in Oxford and New York, it is aimed at professionals all round the world in commerce and industry, government and international organizations, as well as academics interested in public policy.

Editorial Board

Responsibility for the contents of *The World Economy* lies with the co Editors, Peter Oppenheimer, a Fellow of Christ Church, University of Oxford, and Ingo Walter, Gitlow Professor of Economics and Finance at the Graduate School of Business Administration, New York University, and Loudon Professor of International Business at the Institut Européen d'Administration des Affairs (INSEAD), Fontainbleau. The Managing Editor is Hugh Corbet, the Director of the Trade Policy Research Centre, London. The editors are assisted by advisory members of the Editorial Board.

Subscriptions

Set out below are the subscription rates to the journal for non-members of the Centre in 1989:

For institutions it is £61.00 (UK) and US$120.00 (USA, Canada and Japan).

For individuals it is £26.00 (UK) and US$52.00 (USA, Canada and Japan).

In other countries the subscription is the equivalent in convertible currencies at the time of payment of £73.20 for institutions and £31.20 for individuals.

Enquiries about subscriptions to the journal only, and/or sample or single copies, should be addressed either to the Journals Department, Basil Blackwell Ltd, 108 Cowley Road, Oxford OX4 1JF, United Kingdom, or to the Journals Department, Basil Blackwell Inc., Box 1320, Murray Hill Station, New York 10156, United States of America.

List of Major Volumes

SET OUT below are some major volumes that have been published for the Trade Policy Research Centre.

Alasdair MacBean and V.N. Balasubramanyam, *Meeting the Third World Challenge*, second edition (London: Macmillan, 1978; and New York: St Martin's Press, 1978) 288 pp.

M.M. Kostecki, *East-West Trade and the GATT System* (London: Macmillan, 1979; and New York: St Martin's Press, 1979) 170 pp.

Fritz Machlup, Gerhard Fels and Hubertus Müller-Groeling (eds), *Reflections on a Troubled World Economy: Essays in Honour of Herbert Giersch* (London: Macmillan, 1983; and New York: St Martin's Press, 1983) 422 pp.

Richard Pomfret, *Mediterranean Policy of the European Community: A Study of Discrimination in Trade* (London: Macmillan, 1986) 128 pp.

Carl McMillan, *Multinationals from the Second World: Growth of Foreign Investment by Soviet and East European Enterprises* (London: Macmillan, 1987) 220 pp.

Copies of the following two titles are now only obtainable from the Centre.

John Black and Brian Hindley (eds), *Current Issues in Commercial Policy and Diplomacy* (London: Macmillan, 1980;

and New York: St Martin's Press, 1980) 148 pp.

Richard Dale, *Anti-dumping Law in a Liberal Trade Order* (London: Macmillan, 1980; and New York: St Martin's Press, 1980) 244 pp.

Forthcoming Publications

Alan Peacock and Hans Willgerodt (eds), *Germany's Social Market Economy: Origins and Evolution* (London: Macmillan, for the Trade Policy Research Centre)

Alan Peacock and Hans Willgerodt (eds), *German Neo-liberals and the Social Market Economy* (London: Macmillan, for the Trade Policy Research Centre)

In the first volume, seventeen original essays, dealing with a wide range of contemporary economic problems, have been selected to express the views of a group of German liberal economic and legal thinkers who came to prominence as a result of their influence on, and participation in, post-war economic policy in the Federal Republic of Germany. The group, because of their commitment to designing an appropriate economic and legal order or system, based on liberal economics, became known as the Ordo-liberals.

The companion volume is a collection of ten essays by internationally known authors representing a wide range of contempory liberal thought. The authors consider not only the philosophy of the Ordo-liberals and their concept of the social market economy; they are also concerned with the contribution of the Ordo-liberals to policy formation.

These two volumes are about a distinctly German contribution to economic thought which is little-known in the English-speaking world.